The
Shifty
Lad
and the Tales he Told

The Shifty Lad

and Lad

the Tales he Told

CELTIC FOLK STORIES

RETOLD BY P. L. SNOW

Floris Books

First published by Floris Books in 2010

British CIP Data available
ISBN 978-086315-764-6
Printed in Great Britain
by Bell & Bain Ltd, Glasgow

Mixed Sources
Product group from well-managed
forests and other controlled sources
www.fsc.org Cert no. TT-COC-002769
© 1996 Forest Stewardship Council

To my parents, with love and everlasting thanks

Once again I would like to thank Christopher Moore and the people at Floris Books for their help and encouragement.

Most of these tales I have known since childhood, have gathered along the way or have heard from storytellers in storytelling clubs, and similar places, all over these islands (and beyond). But I would like to mention Dora Broome's wonderful collection *Fairy Tales from the Isle of Man* for the story included here as *A Moon of Gobbags*. Another excellent book that I referred to for some of the more out-of-the-way aspects of Scottish folklore is *The Scots Book* by Ronald Macdonald Douglas.

CONTENTS

THE SHIFTY LAD

Shifty he was indeed as a lad, in and out of trouble the day long and his feet dancing over the crab-pools at the shore, or leaping over the heather; his red hair like a flame in the bracken on the braeside, light and fleet as any deer. All the long hours of daylight he would be out at play; if not on the hills or down at the shore, he would be building castles out of the peats in the stack at the head of the house, and he would sit in his fortress and repel all enemies, covered in the peat-dust so that he looked more like a creature from under the earth than a Christian soul upon it. His eyes shone like blue stones out of the dust and the stoor coating his face, and all his friends would gather round to listen to his tales and stories, for he was as full of them as he was ploys and stratagems for mischief and trouble.

He was sitting one day in the peat-stack castle, when he looked thoughtful and not at all like a young boy any more. His features were sharper and more knowing somehow, like a fox.

"I shall be a grown man soon," he said, "and I shall have to earn a living. And I have the mole of good luck in my left oxter. What would my mother say to thievery now? Sure, I would only take from those who could afford to lose. I would not take from those with nothing. It would be no more than fair and just to spread the good things in life a little further around than only in the houses of the rich. There's honour enough in that."

But Shifty's mother was far from happy.

"Do you call that a fit calling for a man?" she demanded. "By jings, if your father were alive he would have something to say on the matter. To think that a son of mine ..."

Her voice became an angry mutter as she swept the floor the way she would sweep the bristles right off the brush. But then Shifty said: "I tell you what, Mother, here's the way of it now. When you go to the kirk on Sunday, the first craft that you hear spoken of on your way out, that'll be the craft I follow. Is that good enough for you, now?"

She turned and looked at him, her lips as tight pressed together as two mill stones, and then she said: "You'd do yourself more good to come into the kirk yourself."

She paused, and said at last: "The first craft I hear spoken of on my way out of the kirk, is that it? Well, all right. We'll go by that. Away with you now. I'm too busy to be bothering with you."

Well, that Sunday, Shifty squatted down behind the kirk wall, waiting for them to come out. He could hear the singing inside and wild and keening it sounded. At last, the door opened and the people started to come out, blinking in the sunlight like calves out of the byre on a spring morning.

At last here she came. Wait, she turned! It was the Factor's wife behind her. Would they start talking about trades that a young man might follow? No; she was coming on.

She came closer till she was nearly at the gate. Then, Shifty leaped up and waved his hands, shouting: "Thievery! Thievery! Thievery!"

At first she looked as though the devil himself had appeared out of the ground at her feet, and herself the one he'd come for. She opened her mouth wide with the shock. Then, seeing Shifty, she looked relieved. But then, when she took in the words he had shouted, her face went grey, and she leaned on the kirk wall for support. When she spoke, she had no idea what she was saying: it came out of some deep place within her.

"You will end your days of thievery hanging from the bridge in Baile Cliath in Erin," she said.

"Come now mother," he said, "remember our bargain. The first craft you heard of when you came out of the kirk on Sunday; mind now!"

"Oh, I mind it right enough," she said, "and the devil mend you."

She turned and went away down the road to their house, bent like an old *cailleach*.

Shifty watched her go, and could it be a wisp of sadness crossing his face? It wasn't there long, anyway.

Well, that's done. She'll have to abide by her word," he said: "And

I'm away to find the Black Rogue of Achnalone!" He laughed and jumped in the air and kicked his heels together.

No-one in that part of the country saw Shifty for many a long day after that. But one day towards the end of the year, with frost on the ground and a mantling of snow on the high hilltops, here was Shifty coming along with a barrow-load of fodder. And this was the tale he told.

The Black Rogue of Achnalone

"Nothing to eat on the table and nothing to drink in the house! And it's myself is to blame for walking the road with the Black Gallows Bird of Achnalone." So spoke the wife of the Black Rogue, as they made their way along the road.

"Such is the fortune of the open road, woman," the Black Rogue answered. "You'll have a full enough belly by this evening. You'll see."

"Aye, but will it be food it'll be full of?" she said, and the bitterness in her voice almost cut him.

"Well, and what else? A fine pair of twins, maybe? Sons to learn the trade of the Black Gallows Bird?"

She gave him a push away from her, but her mood was not quite so dark as it had been. She was a handsome woman, her eyes as grey as the winter sea, but where her hair was once as black as a raven's wing, it was threaded through here and there with silver, and the lines between her eyebrows and beside her mouth were deeper now. As for the Black Rogue; he was a tall, thin man, spare as a lath, with eyes as black as sloe berries and them for ever moving from side to side under deep black eyebrows, and the hair of his head crow-black. He wore a black coat with silver buttons, and there were silver buckles on his shoes that sparkled like flint as he walked with dancing steps through the world.

Everybody knew that the Black Rogue of Achnalone was the rascal behind most of the evil doings in that part of the world, but there was never a body could prove anything one way or the other, and so he went his way untouched as yet by any law of God or man.

Shifty caught up with them, and he gave the Black Rogue a brave cry of greeting.

"And who are you at all, to come shouting my name across the glen?" the Black Rogue said angrily, looking round to left and right and behind to see if others were on the road.

"I'm the lad to learn your trade, and fit indeed am I to learn it," said Shifty. The Black Rogue's wife looked him up and down, and she said: "Aye, you have the look of a boy whose feet hardly touch the ground. What way do you think you're a fit man to follow my man and his work?"

"Try me!" said Shifty simply, and he smiled. That smile melted the woman's heart a little, for she said to her man: "You could do worse than to try him, at least. Give him a job to do and see how well he does it."

"I was thinking the same," the Black Rogue said, still gruff and unsure of this bright young lad in front of him.

At that moment, they became aware of movement on the road, and with a 'Wheesht!' the Black Rogue huckled them all off the road and into the heather. Round the corner came a man leading a sheep on a rope.

"Now," said the Black Rogue, "if ye can take that mannie's sheep and not touch a hair of his head, I'll give you a trial as an apprentice."

"Easy enough," said Shifty, and started forward.

"Wait the now," the Black Rogue said, pulling him back by the shoulder. "You can do it barefoot, maybe?"

"Easier still," said Shifty, and pulled the brogues off his feet. Keeping his head low, he ran away round the corner of the road ahead of the man with the sheep, and left one of his brogues on the crown of the road.

Soon enough, the fellow arrived, and picked up the shoe, which was a good one, and would have fitted him well.

"A good shoe for a one-legged man," he said, wistfully, and let it lie. Shifty, from his hiding place in the roadside, picked up the shoe, put it in his bag and cut ahead again, round the next corner, and left his other brogue on the crown of the road. It was not long before the fellow arrived at the shoe.

"Well, if this isn't the twin of the other back the way, I'll eat you, little sheep, bones, teeth and wool, so I will!" So said the fellow, but he was puzzled how to keep his sheep safe while he ran back to fetch the first shoe. Shifty emerged on to the road, as if he had just come the opposite way.

"You'll do, my friend," said the shepherd: "Hold this shoe and look after this sheep while I go and find its brother on the road behind me. Will you do that?"

"You've lost the sheep's brother?" asked Shifty, all innocence.

"It's the shoe's brother I mean," said the shepherd, and he handed the rope with the sheep at the other end of it to Shifty, and the brogue. Off he went to find the first shoe, which he would spend a long time searching for, as it was in Shifty's bag. Shifty put his brogues back on his feet, and led the sheep to the Black Rogue who had watched this episode with approval.

"Aye, you'll do for a trial, anyway," said the Black Rogue, and he, Shifty, wife and sheep all went the quick way over the hill to the wee town at the lochside, to sell the sheep.

That night, all three sat in a quiet window corner in the change house, or inn, eating and drinking their fill from the profits made from the sale of the sheep. There were a lot of folk packed into the room, and the talk was loud and merry as the good ale and whisky went round.

"Eat up and drink hearty," the Black Gallows Bird said. "Do you take strong drink and spirituous liquor, now?"

"That depends on who pays the round," Shifty replied.

"As long as it's no yourself, I suppose," the wife remarked acidly. Shifty looked at her, as humble as a schoolboy.

"A generous purse makes for good companionship, but a thrifty husbandman reaps the greater rewards," he said, as if reciting a lesson.

"Tut! You talk like the minister's parrot!" she said.

"I got a good price for the minister's parrot at Paddy's Market," Shifty said. They all three laughed at that, even the woman.

"A lad after my own heart," the Black Rogue said, and his wife muttered something about hoping that he was not after everything that belonged to her man. The Black Rogue paid her no attention, and said: "Ah, we'll get on like chestnuts roasting," and he shook

Shifty by the hand. Shifty made a great play of having one finger missing after shaking the Black Gallows Bird's hand, and they all laughed again.

At that moment, the shepherd whose sheep they had sold came into the change house. He looked around, scratching his head. The Black Rogue vanished beneath the table and Shifty was out of the window and looking in, all in a single movement, light as a hare's foot on a tussock.

"Is there a man here called or known as or alias The Black Rogue of Achnalone, sometimes cried the Black Gallows Bird?" the shepherd called into the crowded, smoky room. The Black Rogue, under the table, gritted his teeth and cursed at hearing his name so loud in a small room. However, there were few who would give up the Black Rogue to his enemies or victims, for fear of what he would do to any tale-bearer. People shook their heads and gave no sign.

The shepherd turned at the doorway and said: "It's just I was told he was here, see. I wanted a word wi' him about a sheep I'm missing. I was told he might be able to put me in the way of finding it?"

No-one in the change house gave word or sign even of having heard the man.

"Eh well," he sighed, and he was gone. Shifty came back in through the window and the Black Gallows Bird crawled out from under the table.

"Is that him away?" the Black Rogue whispered. His wife nodded: "Aye. Whisht! He'll no be far down the road yet."

"Well, I think we'll be giving you a trial, young fellow," the Black Rogue said, clapping Shifty on the back.

"Another mouth to feed!" the wife said, but Shifty gave her his broadest, brightest smile, and her frown faded away for a while.

How the Shifty Lad Went to Work

"Up with you now, my Shifty Lad!"

Shifty rubbed the sleep from his eyes and looked through blinking eyes towards the window. It was Samhain, the Celtic New Year that comes at the end of October, and not yet light, but the Black Gallows Bird was shaking him awake.

"Come on, splash some water in your face and let's be away. There's work for the likes of you and me this Samhain!"

"What like of work is this that can't wait for the sun to rise?" said Shifty, pulling on his breeks in the chill of the late autumn morning.

"Do you know who was away to the market with a herd of cows to sell yesterday? The richest farmer in these hills and glens; perhaps even the richest man in Scotland."

"So he'll be home again with a lot of money, no doubt?" said Shifty through a yawn.

"A great kist full of gold and silver! Man, it'll be the making of us, and it will spoil his Samhain! But we can't help that. Come on! This is no time to bide in your bed."

There was just time for the two rascals to drink a cup of tea and eat a bowl of porage standing by the kitchen fire before setting out up the road towards the farmer's house.

"Now this is the way of it," the Black Rogue explained: "You and I will clamber up on to the roof and in through the skylight. There we can wait until the whole household is asleep, and then, down from the loft we go and pick up the guineas and sovereigns. Ah, it's a grand life, Shifty, my lad!"

The journey to the farmer's house took them over two big hills and through a dark glen where crows and ravens wheeled and called hoarse warnings to them against a life of crime. They moved so fleet and softly that their feet hardly left a print in the snow on the higher slopes of the hills, and never a blade of frosty grass bent under their heels.

When the house came into view, it sat in the middle of green fields where cows grazed peacefully. Smoke rose from the chimney like the promise of welcome and warmth. Shifty and the Black Rogue settled down in the heather to wait for the darkness to fall. Sure enough, the day dimmed soon at that time of year, and the owls began to call. Shifty and the Black Rogue made their way carefully following the hedgerows, to the house, making sure that no-one saw them. Light as a pair of shadows they took their way, each man hardly disturbing the grass beneath his feet as they stepped nimbly over the field to the house. Nobody saw them arrive, and the pair of them climbed up on to the roof nimbly as squirrels, and in they went through the skylight.

"Now," said the Black Rogue, "we'll get some rest. When they're all sleeping, we'll go down and do the job we came to do."

The Black Rogue used to make this boast; that if a rope was slung from iron ring on the quayside to a boat in the harbour, he could sleep sound on that rope, and waken any time he chose. He made himself comfortable on some old sacks, and was soon asleep.

"Ah, but I'm not so quick to drowse," thought Shifty, and wondered what entertainment or improvement he could make to the situation. In the lapel of his jacket were a needle and thread against the need for a quick repair, and this fell under his fingers as he ran his hands over his pockets to find a good employment for the period of waiting. A plan formed in his mind as quick as a ripple spreads in a pool when a duck takes flight. With agile fingers, he stitched the Black Rogue's coat tail to the heap of sacks on which he rested, so lightly that the Black Rogue slept through the operation.

That wee task accomplished, he took a nut from his pocket and cracked it between his teeth, for, as he explained to himself, he never yet passed a Samhain night without cracking a nut. And after that nut, he took and cracked another and another after that, while the Black Rogue slept sound on the sacks.

"What's this?" the farmer said, below in his chamber. "Someone cracking nuts in my loft! I will not be having that!"

He swung his legs out of his bed and shouted: "Come down out of that, you, whoever you are! I have a gun here, and it's loaded!"

He did indeed have a gun, and it was loaded with shot and tin tacks and old buttons. The Black Rogue jumped up at the clatter below him, and made for the skylight, but with his train of sacks, he was slowed down in his movements. He muttered and cursed, not knowing whether to free his coat or the skylight catch first. Shifty kept himself back in the shadows, and watched the Black Rogue climb out of the window dragging his sacks behind him, and he heard the discharge of a gun in the yard. The house was all in an uproar now, and servants and people were running out into the yard to see what all the stramash was about. Shifty silently lifted the trap door and let himself down lightly into the bosom of the house. It was not long before he found the kist full of silver and gold, and he made his way out of the house, away from all the noise. He had calculated that the Black Rogue would draw all the attention to himself with the train of sacks sewn to his coat-tails, and would lead the chase away from the house, the gold and Shifty himself. What was his surprise, when he ran full tilt into the arms of a lassie who worked as a servant in the household.

"Quick," he said: "the house is robbed! Take the kist and hide it!"

"I cannae," said she: "I've the puddings to watch!"

"Oh well, I'll do it myself, then!" said Shifty, and sped out of the house and into the shadows, soon leaving all the noise of guns firing, people screaming and angry shouting behind him.

Now a heavy kist of stout wood and iron locks and hinges is an unhandy thing to have to carry a long way, and it did not take Shifty long to find a barrow and a pile of fodder to put over the kist, the way that he could go home at his leisure and no questions asked about his cargo.

Meanwhile, it went badly for the Black Rogue, for they soon caught him, and there were a lot of scores to settle and a lot of bad feeling stacked up against him. The folk there dealt faithfully enough with the Black Rogue of Achnalone. He would rob and steal no more. Shifty watched the proceedings through the gap in a hawthorn hedge, and a shiver of horror ran through him from the crown of his head to his toes. Then it was up and away with him with his barrow load.

The Shifty Lad in Erin

Shifty took the long way, round the hills, whistling as he went, and when he arrived at the bothy where the Black Rogue and his wife stayed, he crept up to the window and listened before he went in.

"Who's there?" cried the Black Rogue's wife: "Why, Shifty! My wee angel, I feared you were dead!" the Black Rogue's wife hugged him to her and kissed his face. It was a bit more than Shifty expected, and he wriggled out of her embrace like a weasel through a hole.

"I've something for you here," said Shifty, showing her the kist. He fetched in the box, blowing the dust of the fodder off it. He fetched a crowbar and soon had the lock dangling by a single rusty screw. Then, they lifted the lid, and what a sight met their eyes. Guineas, sovereigns, marks, crowns, coins from France, coins from places they had never heard of, all in good silver and gold.

"Where's himself?" The Black Rogue's wife asked. "He'll be delighted with this, so he will!"

"He'll not be coming."

"What? Have they lifted him at last? Have I got to go to the city to talk to him through the prison bars? Is that what you're telling me?"

"No" said Shifty. "It's worse nor that."

A soft low moan grew in her breast and grew louder and louder, as she rocked to and fro in her misery. Louder and louder grew her wailing, until Shifty was afraid people would come running. He put his arm about her shoulders, and spoke soothingly to her through her sobs and weeping.

"We'll carry on, you and me," he said quietly. "We'll make a great team the pair of us, just you wait and see."

Her moaning and weeping quietened and she blew her nose and wiped away tears.

"You and me carry on, is it? The two of us, a great team! Get out of here, Shifty Lad. I never want to lay eyes on your foxy face ever again. Go on, get out!"

"You'll maybe feel different in the morning," Shifty began, but she took up a carving knife and shrieked at him to get out. And so, with nothing but the clothes he stood up in and a pocketful of golden guineas, Shifty fled the bothy where the Black Rogue had lived, and ran into the night, with the woman's grief loud in his ears as he ran.

It was but a short while after that he was standing on the quayside, shaking the dust of Scotland from his brogues, and waiting to climb into the boat that would ferry him across the Moyle Stream to the green land of Erin.

For the first days, he travelled through the country, getting used to the land and finding out its ways; listening to the tales told at camp fires and in the drinking houses and getting himself used to the ways of the people. One thing he did, though, before carrying on with his travels through Ireland, was to take a handful of guineas and bury them safely under an oak tree in a field not far from the first town he reached. This would be his emergency supply, only to be touched in times of the greatest distress. The rest he kept in a hidden pocket, and he tried to forget the buried store. Sooner or later, well he knew, he would have to start at his trade, for the guineas that he carried would not hold out for ever. And one day indeed, in a big town lying in the lee of a fine castle, he reached into his pocket to find the last one spent. Charity would have to do now until he could get back on his feet. The sound of a spoke-shave drawn along a piece of wood came to him from the back of a house nearby, so he knew a carpenter lived there. He went over to try his luck.

"Sir, would there be any room at your table for a poor boy?" he asked the grumpy-looking fellow who answered the door.

"How poor?" the carpenter gruffly demanded.

"Poor as the bees."

"The bees is rich enough as long as the flowers bloom," said the carpenter, and would have shut the door. Shifty was too quick with a reply.

"True for you! And they pay taxes to a queen."

"Taxes!" the carpenter bellowed. "Don't talk to me about taxes! Amn't I destroyed with paying taxes here and taxes there, and meself with a hardly a crumb left over! Taxes! Yah!"

He had emerged from his house now, and was almost dancing with rage and frustration in the street.

"What's that," Shifty said. "You don't have enough to eat?"

"Enough to eat!" the carpenter began his angry dance all over again. "If there's anything between my belly and my backbone it's nothing but God's good air!"

"Well," said Shifty. "If that wouldn't stop the clock! If that wouldn't cross a horse's eyes! A man like yourself, a craftsman and master of his trade, with an empty table! And there's kitchens and cellars over beyond that are so full of good victuals that they wouldn't notice if half of them trickled out of the window."

The carpenter stood still and looked closely at Shifty. It was, after all, true enough that a castle on the hill not far away had well-stocked pantries and larders. Shifty had learned this from one of the cooks whom he had met in an ale-house not two days since.

"Full of good victuals, says you," said the carpenter. "And who is to organize this trickling out of the window of these aforementioned groceries?"

"Why, you!" Shifty answered simply.

"Me? Why me?"

"Well, and who else? Is it hungry you are truly, or do you just like to complain?"

"I'm the carpenter is who I am."

"Good. Fine so. You'll have the tools to do the job!"

"Will I so?"

"You will so."

"Well then I will!"

"Spoken like a hero!" Shifty clapped the carpenter on the back. "Now, let's get up to the castle."

"Wait now! Wait now! What's this you're suggesting? The castle?"

Shifty gave a great sigh of disappointment and let his shoulders slump in dejection.

"Ah, and I thought it was a hero I was talking to, and a brave man. And all the time it was just another fellow putting on the poor mouth. Ah well. It can't be helped." And he turned to go. The carpenter ran a few steps after him.

"But this is the castle you're talking about, man! You can't just go walking in there and help yourself and stroll out again!"

"You're right," said Shifty. "We'll need a hammer, a saw, a length of rope, a chisel, and a deal of other tools, too!"

"But you can't just go cutting and chopping your way in there in broad daylight!"

"You're right. That's right! Ah, you're the man of penetration all right. We'll wait until dark. Night-time's the time for dark and dismal deeds! You're a man who knows the world all right. You must tell me all about your adventures when we get back to your house for the banquet."

The carpenter's expression changed a little. New possibilities were beginning to dawn in his mind.

"Banquet?" he murmured.

"There are cheeses and hams; loaves of sweet white bread; sausages and puddings as fat as your thighs; bottles of wine; red wine, white wine ..."

Shifty's picture grew in the carpenter's imagination. He added to it.

"Bottles of ale and stout and porter; pickled onions ..."

"Pickled onions as big as your head!"

"But will there be any mustard, now?" the carpenter demanded. "For if there isn't, I'm not going."

"Mustard! Of course there'll be mustard. Mustard; pickles of all kinds ..."

The carpenter fell silent a while. Then he headed purposefully towards the castle, saying: "Come on. We'll go now."

Shifty ran after him and grabbed his arm.

"We will not! We'll wait until dark. Then, we'll go up and see what's waiting for us up there."

"Fair enough," said the carpenter. "Will you come inside while we're waiting?"

How the Castle was Robbed

A few days later, the castle cook and the royal vintner were giving a list of missing items to the King's equerry, or Shanacal as he was called.

"And what else is missing?" the Shanacal asked.

"Three hams and five loaves of bread," said the cook.

"Six bottles of wine, assorted, of the best," said the vintner.

"And how did the miscreants get in?" the Shanacal asked.

"Through a skylight, your honour, which they made some shifts to repair before leaving," said the cook. The Shanacal looked thoughtful.

"So they tried to repair the damaged skylight before they left, did they? Well now look here. It's my guess that they'll try that way in again."

He called one of the castle guards over.

"Now, here's what we'll do: we'll have a barrel of soft pitch waiting under the skylight, and whoever comes in that way will find himself stuck fast, and we'll have the rascal."

The guard turned to follow his orders, but the Shanacal called him back.

"There's no need to worry the King with this business," he confided close in the guard's ear. "After all, he's away at his castle in Baile Cliath. We'll take care of it."

That night, Shifty and the carpenter made their way stealthily to the castle grounds, to a place in the wall where a tree drooped a low branch. Over they went, and made their way to the skylight over the royal pantries. The roof here was low, and they climbed up easily.

"Right. You first," whispered Shifty.

"Me? Why me?"

"Don't waste time arguing! In you go."

The catch was broken, for they had broken it, and the skylight opened easily enough. Shifty took the rope from round his shoulder and made it fast to a chimney stack.

"Lower away," whispered the carpenter, and Shifty slowly paid out the rope with the carpenter on the end of it. But then the Carpenter found himself up to the waist in soft pitch.

"Help! Pull me up! I'm stuck in something! Quick, get me out!"

Shifty pulled and heaved, but the weight of the carpenter and the barrel of pitch was too much for him. There was nothing for it. The guards were on their way, and Shifty had to scramble down off the roof and run light-footed up to the wall and over it, and back to the carpenter's house.

When the carpenter's wife learned what had happened, she was beside herself.

"Where have they taken him?" she kept asking, but Shifty did not know at all where the carpenter was being kept.

"Hush now. You must be brave," he told her, trying to dry her tears with a piece of cloth that had been wrapped round a stolen cheese.

"He's not much of a man, but he's all I have," she moaned. "What will they do to him?"

"Be brave, now. Be brave," Shifty said soothingly.

"Ah, ye keep saying that! What good is it? No good at all!"

The street outside was suddenly full of movement and life. Shifty looked out of the window, and saw a troop of guards from the castle, with the carpenter, a much bruised and bleeding wreck of a man, being held up by two stout soldiers. The carpenter's wife, looking out of the window, would have screamed if Shifty had not put his hand over her mouth.

"Wheesht!" he commanded, "not a sound, now!"

"Now hear ye all present," said a voice outside. "This malefactor was discovered breaking in to the castle and stealing food from His Majesty's table. If anyone here can put a name on this man here, ye are to declare it now."

The carpenter's wife let a cry out of her that fell into the street like a wounded bird.

"Who spoke?" the Sergeant of the Guard demanded. One of his

men pointed to the carpenter's house as the source of the noise. The Sergeant came and beat his great fist three times on the door.

"Who spoke in here?" he said.

"I did," said Shifty. "I hit my thumb with a hammer. Look, it'll be all right. I'll have a blue thumbnail, that's all."

The Sergeant turned away to his men.

"Ah, we'll find nothing here. Away to the market place with him, and swipe off his head."

"Did you hear that?" the carpenter's wife said. "Oh, they'll kill him. They'll kill him!"

"Don't you worry. I'll get away down to the market place and steal him back for you," Shifty assured her.

Sad to tell, by the time Shifty got down to the market place, the Carpenter was no more.

The Shifty Lad and the Princess

It began to work like a worm in his mind that the people who came into close contact with Shifty generally suffered for it. There was the shepherd who lost his lamb, the Black Rogue, and there was the greedy carpenter. There were their wives, too, and the sorrow they had. This was not a comfortable thing to consider, and so Shifty began to wonder whether the time had not come after all, to change his ways.

"I will," he said to himself, "I'll change the ways of my thievery. I must become a different sort of thief altogether. But I'll need a start."

So he resolved to go and dig up the buried store of guineas. With this, he would buy himself good clothes of the best, and look for a position worthy of a gentleman. It was in this way that he arrived, dressed like a noble young lording, in the town of Baile Cliath.

Now, the King of Erin had many castles, and one of them was in the town of Baile Cliath. This was where he was staying at the moment when the Shifty Lad arrived, all in his finery.

"Come over here now," said the King to his daughter the princess, as he looked out of a window in the castle at the market place: "Tell me what you make of this young fellow below."

The princess looked down, and saw Shifty, wandering among the stalls in the market, sampling an apple here, sniffing at a fish there.

"Well," she said at length, "he's a young man without much in the way of riches, but a good opinion of himself."

"You're right about the good opinion," said the King, "but how can you tell about the riches?"

"His clothes are good enough, but he's walking on his own two feet."

"What does that tell you?"

"He's not riding a horse of any colour, and he has no servant to search the market place on his behalf."

The King stroked his beard thoughtfully.

"Your observations tally with my own," he said, "but do you know this: he's staying at the best inn and eating the best they can get him. So they tell me."

"Ah, it's a wonderful thing entirely to be a King, and have such powerful sources of information," the princess said with an ironic lift of the eyebrow.

"Call them by their right name. Spies is what they are," the King said, and continued: "But what would a fellow like that, with a Scottish tongue on him, be doing in this town?"

"Will your spies not find that out?"

"There's others that can find out more things than they can, and with less trouble."

And in that way, the princess, dressed like a lady, but not as richly as a princess, went down to meet Shifty, to find out all she could about him. She saw him walking alongside the river, and put herself in the way where his footsteps would take him. As he passed, she dropped her handkerchief. He retrieved it at once, and ran after her.

"Excuse me," he said as he came level with her, "did you drop this?"

"I think not," she said haughtily, and walked on.

"Are you sure now?" Shifty insisted, following her.

"What way would I not know my own things?" she said, a little crisply. It had not been her intention to engage him in conversation right away, but to get a look at him, and cross his path another day. There was more to their first conversation than she had meant to allow, and it made her a little cross with herself that her plan was working out differently.

"Oh, it's a wise girl that knows her own things, right enough," said Shifty, "but you see, there's something about this handkerchief." And he smelled it, as though it were a flower.

"Something about it?" she asked, and looked at him more closely. He was a handsome young man, right enough.

"The smell of it, you see. Do you know the smell of meadowsweet in the summer? Or, wait! Is it honeysuckle? Yes, I think it's honeysuckle."

"You know the scents of flowers, anyway," the princess said, deciding to allow the conversation to go where it would, and be faithful to her father's commission to find out more about the young man.

"I think I do, and there are worse things to talk about. But it was the scent of your hair that makes me wonder if this handkerchief is yours after all?"

The princess was on the verge of giving his face a good slap! Who was this impudent fellow talking about the scent of her hair, at all?

"It's bold you are to talk about my hair in a place where anyone walks!" she said with a face blossoming into poppy red.

"I meant no offence," said Shifty, "but you see I caught a waif smell of honeysuckle on the air as you passed, so I wondered ..."

"You're sure it wasn't meadowsweet in the summer?"

"I'm sure it smells as sweet as the one who dropped it, whoever she is." And he looked around, as though trying to see the owner of the handkerchief.

"Oh," said the princess, "I made a mistake. It is mine after all." So saying, she took it brusquely from his hand.

"Glad to be of service," said Shifty, and bowed and turned to go.

"Not so fast," called the princess. "I'm not in the habit of seeing young men walk away from me so quickly." She was regretting having taken on this charge, but fascinated by this young fellow in spite of herself.

"With one as beautiful as yourself, how could it be otherwise?"

"So why away so hasty?"

"Business of my own."

A detestable thought occurred to her: this young man might be thinking that she was after his money! She spoke hotly to him, with a flame in her eye.

"You think it's your gold and silver I'm after, don't you! Look at this ring, young man! How much gold and silver would tempt the owner of such a ring?"

"Fine workmanship, surely," said Shifty, "and therefore you must be of noble blood. In which case, I would not have you condescend to me further. Good day!"

With that, Shifty walked away from her smartly, without a backward look. The princess stamped her foot.

"I let him get away from me without even learning his name!" she thought: "Well, he won't have a second chance to do that to me!"

Shifty was thinking as he walked, too.

"Here's a mystery! A lovely young woman taking an interest in me that all her haughtiness and pride could not conceal. I'll dodge between these bushes, and double back and follow her, and find out a few things on my own account."

So he did. He followed her to a high wall, in the midst of which was a low door. She opened it and went in, leaving Shifty on the path outside. A little farther on was a growth of ivy that let him climb to the top of the wall, and drop down into a rich garden on the other side. He made his way softly and lightly to a bush beside a bower where two people were talking. It was the King and the princess. He was seated in the bower, and she was pacing crossly to and fro, twisting the handkerchief angrily between her fingers.

"So you let him slip away. He was too slick for you, eh?" the King said, smiling.

"He shan't get the chance to do it again!" she replied.

"Ah, but you see, I think he will."

"What way do you think that at all?"

"I think that because I have not dismissed you from your duty yet."

As Shifty listened to their conversation, it welled up in his mind like a flood that here was the King! And the young woman whom he had accosted was the princess! And now she was being given orders from her father to find out more about none other but himself, the Shifty Lad. Well, he would make himself available to her the first chance that came along.

That chance came two days later. Shifty was sat under a willow beside the river, near the castle, as he had for the hours of daylight since he had overheard the conversation between the princess and her father, thinking that maybe she would chance to come this way looking out for him. Now here she was, with two soldiers walking the length of two full paces behind her, and she ambling along with a flower in her hands.

He waited until her shadow fell across him, then he turned and looked up.

"Ah," he said, "the haughty lady. Or perhaps there's a better name to call you?"

"There is, but I don't know that I want to hear it on your lips," came the reply.

"Well, it seems to me," said Shifty, rising, "that I've found a name for you that is as true as any other."

They spoke quietly, and the soldiers had to strain to hear any of the conversation.

"Shall I tell you the name I picked out for you?" she asked.

"I'm honoured that you think about me enough to give me a name at all," Shifty said, and the shot went home. She coloured as pink as the rose in her fingers.

"Not at all," she said sharply. "When a young man arrives in the town, spending money like a lord, but with no servant to run his errands, people talk, and the talk gets around."

"Even as far as to the ears of the King?"

"What!"

"And to the ears of his beautiful daughter?"

She took a step back and, without turning to the soldiers, said sharply: "Arrest him!"

"Wait, wait, wait!" Shifty said quickly, "I'll go quietly with you and your men, but wouldn't it be better if I walked beside you, as if just talking of this and that and your men followed close behind? It might not be seemly for you to be seen accompanying a criminal, might it?"

And that is how the Shifty Lad came before the presence of the King of Erin.

The Shifty Lad Finds His Fortunes Turn

"What good fortune," the King asked, "brings a handsome and well-to-do young man such as yourself to our shores?"

"I come, Sire, to offer my services."

"We had not looked to find such generosity," said the King, sitting comfortably in the great cushioned chair in the rich chamber. Shifty stood before him, bold but not insolent.

"I will tell you all the truth, Sire. It is true that I have fortune's mark in my left oxter; a mole of good luck. But when I set out on my adventures, I followed the trade, or calling, of a thief ..."

"And what service do you think you might offer a king, Mister Fortunate Thief?" the King demanded, quick and sharp as a dart.

"The talents that make a thief make a good servant to a king," Shifty replied: "nimble fingers and toes; a soft and silent way of moving; a good pair of ears; knowing when to speak and when to say nothing, and quick-wittedness."

"Yet you were caught quickly enough."

"I allowed myself to be caught, Sire, the better to be able to offer my services to you in person. I trust my good fortune to that extent."

"A likely story!" the King said scoffingly. "And now young man, we'll see how lucky you are in stealing your way out of a cell. Take him away."

So Shifty found himself locked in a cold, dark cell, with a wooden bench to sleep on and a cracked jug of water with a stale piece of bread beside it. Shifty looked around his narrow confines, and saw a way to do as the King had told him. When he heard the guard coming on his round with fresh water, he squeezed himself up into the space above the door, and held himself there by pressing his feet against one side and his back and shoulders against the other.

At last the door opened, and the guard came in, looked around, and muttered to himself in disbelief: "He's away!"

Shifty jumped down as easily as a bird and away with him down the cold, dark corridor, and into a shadowy doorway. The guard emerged from the cell and ran up the opposite way, calling for help, for a prisoner had escaped.

At the end of the corridor was the guard's room, and the window was unshuttered. Shifty looked out, and saw the ivy climbing on stout stems up the wall. He scrambled out of the window and up the ivy, as high as he could; though the stems grew thinner the higher he went, and the ground farther and farther away, and a harder drop the higher he climbed.

Luckily, before it became too thin to support his weight, he came to an open window, and dropped lightly into the room. It was small and shadowy, but beyond it, in the next room were voices. Shifty knew the King's voice at once.

"Then don't just stand there gaping like a fish out of water," the King was saying. "Get after him!"

The princess said something that Shifty couldn't quite hear, but the King's response made clear what she was asking.

"Reward? Reward is it! Damn all the reward these fools will get from me! They can't even keep a fellow in a locked room without losing him! I want him here, now, before me!"

Shifty waited until he heard the door in the next room slam, and he slipped quietly in to join the King and the princess. It was she who saw him first, but Shifty raised his finger to his lips. Then he spoke.

"Ahem. Sire, your wish is granted. I present myself to you."

The King was thunderstruck. His face turned deep red, then pale, but gradually regained its healthy colour.

"Well," he said in a soft tone, "here you are indeed. Now, will I throw you back in your cell, or have you stretched on the rack, and then throw you back in your cell?"

"Sire, I hope you'll do neither. But if you wanted a demonstration of my skills, then I think I've given you one already by appearing here before you. If you want a proof of my good faith, well, here I am when I could be away on my toes over the fields. Instead, here I stand, offering my services to you."

For a good wee while, the King's temper and wisdom strove for the upper hand in his soul. One moment he would loosen his sword in its sheath, as if to smite off Shifty's head; the next, he would stroke his beard and look shrewdly at the impertinent young fellow opposite him. At last, he turned his gaze to his daughter, and sat himself down on a cushioned chair.

"How did you know how to find my chambers?" he demanded.

"Sure, that was no more than luck," said Shifty. "I climbed the ivy, and it led me here."

"Ah, the ivy, to be sure. Well, we must get that all torn down. But you think you have something to offer me, hah?"

"I can escape from prisons, I'm the best thief you'll ever meet, and such a fellow could be of great value to you and your Kingdom, I believe."

The King's anger began to rise again.

"D'ye think I employ thieves and scoundrels?" he spluttered, and his hand went back to his sword-hilt.

"I think a good spy needs to be a good thief, and know how to get out of tight places," Shifty replied.

The princess watched her father closely, and she knew that two imps were wrestling in his breast: one was the imp of fury; the other was the imp of laughter. If the imp of fury won the contest, the Shifty Lad would have the head swiped off him within the hour. She waited for the right moment, knowing that everything depended on her getting the exact second right, and — she laughed!

The laughter was infectious, and the King caught it, and laughed too. The King and the princess laughed and laughed; the King with tears running down his face. Then, as the laughter began to die down, again timing the moment as exactly as she could, the princess said:

"Well, you could give him a try, I suppose. There'd be nothing lost in that."

"D'ye think?" said the King, stroking his beard. "Ach well, I suppose we can give him a try, after all. But we'll keep you on a short leash for a wee while yet," he said.

"Thank you, Sire," said Shifty, "I shall do what I can to prove my worth to you."

At the end of an hour, the royal household was assured that the hunt for the runaway prisoner was off, the King was satisfied that there was no danger, and here was a new recruit to the King's council.

Shifty's heart was full. He was still to live by his wits, to be sure, but now as the trusted officer of a king. What's more, he would be close to a very beautiful girl; a princess, no less. The thought filled him with joy. And did she not show some concern for him at a crucial time? Shifty had seen her watching the King, and knew that it was through her intervention that his life was saved. He sought every chance to be near her, doing her little services when he could, picking up things she had dropped, fetching things she had left behind — ah! But could she really be so clumsy and forgetful? Was there not a way she had of looking at him that allowed him to hope that perhaps she, too, felt an inclination of the heart towards him? The last thing I steal, Shifty thought to himself one night, as he lay in his comfortable bed in the castle, will be the heart of the princess. And indeed, it's a fair exchange and no robbery, for hasn't she stolen mine, itself?

The Bridge at Baile Cliath

And so it came about that Shifty and the princess were walking along by the river one day. The river was in full spate with the melting of the winter snows, and cold and foaming. The princess still had the duty of keeping a close eye on the Shifty Lad, and each of them was most happy that she had this commission.

As the sun was beginning to set, they reached the bridge that led over to the castle. Shifty looked thoughtful, and said: "You know, my mother told me that I would end my days of thievery hanging from the bridge at Baile Cliath. I wonder what that would feel like, now."

"Why not try it and see?" said the princess. She slipped off her long silken kerchief, and handed it to him.

"All right," said Shifty, "but be sure and haul me up when I need you to!"

He made a knot in the kerchief and dangled himself from the parapet of the bridge, with the river rushing fast and full below.

"What is it like?" the princess called from above, shouting over the noise of the river.

"It's enough to make me never want to put my hand to thievery ever again!" Shifty shouted back. The sun was almost set, and the darkness and the chill torrent below sent cold shivers running through him.

Not far away, a group of children were playing games. Out of the day's last shadows stepped a stranger all in black, with his head hooded. He approached the children and said: "Do you know the game 'The Castle's On Fire'?"

The children, of course, all knew that game, and a grand game it was, too. They started playing it with great glee in the fading light, and at the climax of the game came the cry: "The castle's on fire, the castle's on fire!"

The princess, having been brought up in a castle, and never mixing with the children of the street, had never played this game; indeed, had never heard of it. When she heard the cry of the children she had no idea that it was no more than a game that they were playing, and ran with all speed to the castle to see what damage there was, and what she could do to help.

"Haul me up now!" yelled Shifty from his uncomfortable position. But the princess was gone. There was nobody to hear his cries.

"Hey!" Shifty shouted. "Heave me back up! My arms are coming out of their sockets!"

As he struggled and kicked to gain purchase to climb back up, he found himself staring into the cold, white face of the Dark Stranger. He was grinning at Shifty, but no warmth was in that grin. He looked hungry and satisfied, all at once. Cold shivers ran like mountain water down Shifty's back at the sight, and he remembered his mother's words of warning.

There was no mistaking who this Dark Stranger was, but Shifty could neither speak his name aloud, nor even name him in the silence of his mind.

"It's I'm the one that will be helping you out of this, my Shifty Lad," he said, and the shadows grew darker and the waters turned black as the sun went down behind the hills. At once, all the strength went out of Shifty's arms, and the last thing he knew was that the princess's kerchief was slipping out of his hands.

The Tales he Told

When he opened his eyes, he was sitting on the top of a high tower, and the Stranger standing beside him. He tried to remember how they had come there, but could make nothing of it. His clothes were dry, however.

"I thought I fell into the river," Shifty said.

"You would have done so had I not caught you," the Dark One said.

"So I am to go with you now?"

"That is the way of it indeed."

Shifty cast about wildly for help. This one, he knew, would not listen to pleas or prayers, and threats were useless. There was no escaping this time, and only the light of day would free him, and that was a long way off.

There was no moon that night, and the stars were veiled by clouds. If there was any hope, he had to compass it in the darkness of all the long, chilly night before him, or he would be bound on the last great adventure, with this dark, hooded stranger as his companion on the mysterious and lonely journey. The stranger's eyes were cold and piercing, and promised no friendship or sympathy. Nothing lay between the Dark Stranger's grim purpose and Shifty but his own wits.

"Well it's my light that has deserted me this day," he said. "Just like poor Donny."

"And who is poor Donny?" the Dark Stranger asked.

"What, you never heard of poor Donny the widow's son, and how he lost his light?" said Shifty, in a tone of great surprise.

"I did not," said the Hooded Stranger, who was ever keen to extend his knowledge of the ways of men and women, for there were mysteries of the human soul that even he had not penetrated.

"Ah, then I must tell you," said Shifty, and this was the first tale that he told.

How Donny Lost His Light

It was a bright September day when Donny the poor widow's son took a basket and set off to gather brambles on the hillside.

"I'll have none but the biggest and sweetest and best for you, Mammy," he called as he set off. His Mammy called after him: "Now ca' canny, Donny! Dinnae be going beyond the Botach Mor."

The Botach Mor was a big standing stone up the braeside, overlooking where the best brambles grew.

"And how should I no go beyond the Botach Mor?" called Donny.

"Today's the Good Folks' Dancing Day and they dinnae like to be interrupted!"

That was true enough. The Good Folk, or the Fairies, as some call them, or the Shee as others call them, were not fond of being spied on in their festivals, and could be very hard on those that they caught.

"Och, I'll be careful, Mammy!" Donny shouted, and went away up the braeside with a leap and a jump, and sure it wasn't long before he had a good pile of brambles in his basket. Now here he stood in the shadow of the Botach Mor, and he could see some of the biggest and sweetest and juiciest brambles growing just beyond where the great grey stone stood.

"Ach, what she doesn't know won't hurt her!" thought Donny, and made his way up towards the biggest of the purple-black berries.

Well, it was just a little further, and just a little further, until Donny found himself near the edge of a wee dingle. In the dingle, he could hear a wonderful music that flooded through him from head to toe, and made him want to dance and sing. He crept a little closer to the edge of the hollow, and looked over.

There below him was a great gathering of the Fairy Folk, dancing and singing to the music of fiddles and pipes and drums. It was all Donny could do to keep still and watch.

The Good Folk were singing as they danced, and the words were:

> "Di-luain, di-mairt
> Di-luain, di-mairt
> Di-luain, di-mairt" —

And they would stamp their feet twice. Well, Donny knew that the Good Folk speak nothing but good Gaelic, and he knew that they were singing:

> "Monday, Tuesday
> Monday, Tuesday
> Monday, Tuesday" —

And he knew that Wednesday comes after Tuesday, and that in Gaelic, Wednesday is Di-Ciadaoin. And so, unable to help himself, the next time the chorus came round of:

> "Di-luain, di-mairt
> Di-luain, di-mairt
> Di-luain, di-mairt" —

He had to join in with:

> "Is di-ciadaoin!"

Everything went silent! The music stopped and the fairy folk all huddled together, pointing up at Donny, and looking very angry. Suddenly, into their midst came a tall and very beautiful lady, all in green and gold; the Queen of the Shee. The Queen spoke to Donny in tones that could accept no denial.

"Donny! Come down here at once!"

Donny, very nervous and shamefaced, made his way down into the hollow, apologizing as he went.

"Silence! Did I bid you speak? I did not!"

Donny hung his head, very afraid of what would come next.

"So, Donny, the widow's son, did you think our singing needed your correction?"

"No, no, I was just ..."

"Did you think your voice was sweeter than our voices?"

"No, no! I'm really sorry ..."

"Then what is your excuse for this vile interruption?"

"No excuse at all, my lady. I was just ..."

"Just so, no excuse at all. Now mark me well, Donny the widow's son. I am going to take away your light. And we'll see how you manage to go through life without it."

She made strange magical movements with her hands over Donny's head, and he could feel something swirling out of him, like a soft breeze. As he did so, the world became all rather puzzling. He gazed about him like a calf on the first day out of the byre after the winter.

"Now go, Donny," said the Queen of the Shee, "but I shall say this before you go. If ever you go to the House of the Wind three times, your light may be restored to you."

Then she sang a strange song that went thus:

"Thrice to the House of the Wind, thrice,
Three the gifts from the Wind's Dwelling.
Twice the cheating half-way, twice,
But all fair at the final telling."

"Now," she commanded, "Go!"

Donny turned to go.

"Wait," called the Queen. "Don't forget your brambles!"

Donny picked up the basket.

"Well, don't just stand there. Go!" ordered the Queen, and Donny made his way out of the dingle and slowly homewards.

When Donny's mother saw him, she almost wept!

"Oh, Donny! You went up the brae on the Good Folk's Dancing Day!"

"Aye, that's right, Mammy!"

"And now they've taken away your light, and it's Dim Donny they'll be calling you!"

It was true. Donny was now dim as the last embers of a cold fire. Still, he had a good heart, and did what he could to help his Mammy about the croft where they lived, and do errands, as long as they weren't too complicated.

One day, he was out gathering firewood, and he found a bright needle, shining in the sunlight.

"Ah, that will be a good thing to take home to Mammy," said Donny to himself, and he picked it up. But how was he to carry it? Nothing better came to Donny's mind than to put it in among the firewood, where, being so thin and smooth, it soon fell out, without Donny noticing.

When he reached home, how happy he was to announce to his Mammy his find, but there was no sign of it among the wood.

"But it was here, I had it!" Donny lamented.

"Ah, Donny, Donny, Donny!" said Mammy, "You haven't even the sense you were born with. Now, if you ever find it again, you must just thread it through a pinch of your shirt's cloth, or into your collar. That way, you won't lose it."

"I'll remember, Mammy," said Donny. And so he did. He was out the next day going a message, when he came upon a wee lost ram.

"Och, the poor wee thing," said Donny. "I'll take it to mammy. She'll know what to do."

Remembering what his Mammy had said, Donny tried to thread the ram's horn through a pinch of his shirt, but the ram was not at all keen to play this game, and left Donny with his shirt torn, and nothing to take home.

"Ah, Donny, Donny, Donny!" said Mammy, shaking her head sadly. "You haven't even the sense you were born with. Now listen: if you find a wee ram, you lift it by its hind legs and fore legs, and hoist it up on to your shoulders, and carry it home that way. Do you see?"

Donny saw perfectly, and he remembered it the next day, when a riderless horse came trotting down the road.

"A horse without a rider!" Donny said to himself: "Mammy will know what to do with such a beast. Now, what was this she said?"

And that was why Donny was next seen trying to gather the horse's hind hooves and fore hooves in each hand, to hoist the great animal up on to his shoulders. Of course, the horse was much surprised by this, and gave Donny a shove into a big black puddle before trotting away.

"Ah, Donny, Donny, Donny," said Mammy, as she took the filthy clothes off Donny's back to wash them. "You haven't the sense you were born with! Now, when you come upon a horse with no rider, you climb on to his back and ride him home. Now, will you remember that?"

Of course Donny remembered fine what Mammy said when he saw a bull in the lane that should have been in the field.

"Oho! I know how to deal with you, sir!" said the bold Donny, and, taking the bull by its long horns, he tried to jump on its back. The bull, of course, was not at all pleased to be treated in this way, holding himself to be a fine creature, and no common beast of burden. And so Donny and the bull began a strange dance, with Donny trying to jump on to the bull's back, and the bull moving away, or shaking him off, and Donny growing more determined at each rebuff.

Now, just at that time, the daughter of the King of Erin was travelling in Scotland. This princess was under a *geis*, which is an obligation that cannot be broken, that she would marry the first man ever to make her laugh. She fondly imagined that this would be a great warrior, or a handsome prince. But now, looking out of the window, she beheld Donny in his struggles to climb aboard the bull's back and ride him like a noble steed. The longer she watched, the more she smiled, and the more she smiled, the more the smile caught her breath into a laugh, and he she was at last, laughing at Donny's efforts.

Then she stopped in alarm.

"Oh no!" she said. "Surely not! Sure, that was just a little giggle and no laugh at all!"

"It was a laugh, Your Highness," said the Shanacal who was travelling with her, "and you'll have to marry him."

And thus it was, and thus it happened, that Donny married the daughter of the King of Erin, and a royal princess came to live in a little wee house in Scotland.

"It seems to me," said the Dark Stranger to Shifty, "that the King's daughter got a poor bargain."

"Ah, no! Not at all!" said Shifty, for the story doesn't end there. This is how it all came out in the end ..."

How Donny Regained His Light

Now Donny's Mammy had to pay rent to the Factor, who
was a cruel, hard man, who would take no excuses. When he
discovered that there was another person living on the property
with Donny and his Mammy, he at once announced that the rent
would have to increase by half a crown a week.

"And where am I to find that?" cried Mammy in despair.

"That's your business," said the Factor, "and it's mine to make
sure you pay it, or out you go!"

"If my father heard you talk like that," said the princess, "you
wouldn't have your head on your shoulders long!"

"Oho!" said the Factor, "and who might your father be?"

Mammy at once tried to stop her from telling, but she was
too late.

"My father," the girl said proudly, "is the King of Erin!"

The Factor stood dumbfounded for a second, and then he
burst into loud, harsh laughter.

"Oh, I'm sorry for you, Mistress," he said to Mammy. "With a
daft son and a crazy daughter-in-law! But rent's rent, and must
be paid!"

Off he went still chuckling to himself like a magpie.

If the rise in rent was a misfortune, the haymaking was a disaster.
The princess had never taken a hand at such work before, and
a poor job she made of it. When the wind blew the night after
haymaking, the stooks that the princess made were all blown over
the hills and far away. Poor Mammy was in a dreadful state.

"No hay for the winter!" she moaned. "What can we do?
What's to be done?"

Just then, who should appear on the road outside the house
but the Spaewife. She was a very wise woman who knew how to

cure sick animals and people. Some said she was in league with the Good Folk, or the fairies, as others call them.

"Wheesht now, Wheesht," she said to Mammy, in a comforting voice. "Now, I'll tell you what is to be done. Someone must go to the House of the Wind to seek reparation for the hay that was lost."

"The House of the Wind," said Mammy, helplessly. "And how ever am I to find my way there, at all?"

"Not you," said the Spaewife. "It's Donny that must go."

"Donny?" cried Mammy. "But he'll never manage a trip like that! You know how it is with him since the Good Folk took away his light!"

"It must be Donny, and none other," said the Spaewife firmly. "Now, Donny, take this ball of yarn, and take one end between your fingers, and let the rest of the ball unwind before you. But be careful to wind it in as you follow it wherever it goes! And when you get to the end of the yarn, you'll be at the Half-Way House. You can rest there, and send the ball of yarn out before you the next day, and when the yarn is all unwound, you'll be before the door of the House of the Wind."

Donny listened very carefully as the Spaewife gave her instructions, though all the while Mammy wrung her hands and muttered: "He'll forget it all! He'll forget it all!"

"Now the door has a hole, right at the heart of it. You put your hand over the hole, and when a voice asks who you are, say that it's Donny come seeking reparation for the hay that was lost."

"It's Donny seeking preparation ..." said Donny.

"Oh, it's no use, you'll have to let me go!" said Mammy, but the Spaewife was adamant.

"No, no! Donny himself and no-one else must go. And it's *reparation*, Donny. You can say that, can't you, now?"

At last Donny got what he had to say, and he set off, letting the ball of yarn unwind before him as he went on his way.

Down the road went the ball of yarn, uphill and down, leaping over streams and up the brae side here, and down the far side there, and Donny running along behind, saying over and over to himself the words that he was to speak at the door of the House of the Wind.

After a long day's journey, and Donny far away from his own country, he found himself at the Half-Way House, where he was welcomed and given a good meal, and a bed for the night.

"Welcome, welcome young man," said the host. "And what brings you here?"

Donny explained that he was on his way to the House of the Wind to seek reparation for the hay that was lost. The host heard this, and gave a look to his wife, and they exchanged a wink, tough Donny didn't see it.

"Well now, Donny, my lad," said the host, "be sure and visit us on the way home, won't you! There'll be a welcome here for you, you can be sure of that!"

Next day, bright and early, Donny set out, following the ball of yarn, now over craggy rocks and up steep mountainsides, until he stood on a high, wind-blown peak, and there, though there were no walls or windows, was a door, with a hole in the centre of it.

Donny remembered what to do, and put his hand over the hole. The wind blew raging around the high summit, and a great voice seemed to fill all the world around him, saying: "WHO'S THAT STOPPING MY BREATH?"

Donny spoke up his lesson clearly, saying: "It's Donny the poor widow's son, come seeking reparation for the hay that was lost."

The wind dropped, and the door opened. There, on the threshold, stood a quern stone, for grinding corn.

"Sure, we have one of those at home," said Donny.

"Not like this, mortal," said a voice from beyond the door. "For you must set this one down beside a bag of corn and say: Grind Quern, Grind! And all your corn will be ground to flour."

Even poor Donny could see what a blessing this would be to his poor mother, so with a word of thanks, he picked it up and made his way to the Half-Way House.

"Now, did you find your way all right, Donny?" asked the host, friendly as a hungry cat.

"I did," said Donny.

"And did you get anything for your trouble?" asked the host, and winked at his wife.

"I got this quern stone," Donny replied. The host scratched his head as he looked at it, and said, "It seems an awful weight to carry all the way home, and it no more than a quern stone such as you have already!" said he.

"Ah, no," said Donny. "Have you got any bags of corn that need ground, for this quern stone here will do the job all by itself!"

The host fetched in a bag of corn, and Donny set the quern stone down beside it.

"Now, watch this," he said: "Grind, Quern, grind!"

In a flash, all the corn was ground into fine flour.

"Now that's a wonderful thing," said the host: "You run along and climb into bed, Donny, and get a good night's sleep. We'll look after your quern stone for you."

But when Donny set off in the morning, the weight he was carrying under his arm was an old, ordinary quern stone, for the host and his wife had hidden away the right one for their own use. This common old quern stone Donny set before Mammy and the princess with great pride.

"Now, just you watch this, Mammy," he said, setting a bag of corn down beside the quern stone.

"Grind, Quern, grind!" he commanded. Nothing happened. He gave it the command again, and still nothing happened.

"Och, Donny," said Mammy, "it's no use at all! That's not reparation for the hay that was lost. That's no more than a lump of stone!"

"Are you sure you're saying the command right?" the princess asked. Donny was growing crosser and crosser, and feeling black-affronted that his prize was no prize at all, but just more lumber to clutter the byre.

"Grind, Quern, grind!" he shouted again, and gave the quern stone a kick, which was unfortunate, for his feet were bare, the quern stone was hard, and the kick did nothing to encourage the thing into action.

It was not long before Donny was making his way over hills and leaping streams, up the braes and down, following the ball of yarn back to the House of the Wind. Once again, he put up at the Half-Way House, and promised to stay with them again on his way back.

Again he found himself on a high, blustery peak, standing before the door. He put his hand over the hole, and again the great voice filled all the air around him.

"WHO'S THAT STOPPING MY BREATH?"

"It's Donny the poor widow's son, seeking reparation for the hay that was lost!"

"AGAIN? YOU TROUBLE ME AGAIN, MORTAL?"

"That quern stone that you gave me didnae work," Donny explained. There was a sudden gust of wind, and the door opened again. On the threshold this time was a young pony, all black and white one side, and chestnut red the other. The pony trotted out and approached Donny in a friendly way, nuzzling up against him.

"GIVE THE PONY THE COMMAND: SHAKE, CUDDY, SHAKE. HE WILL GIVE YOU REPARATION ENOUGH," said the great voice, and Donny happily led the pony away.

At the Half-Way House, the host and his wife were delighted to see Donny again.

"My, that's a braw-looking beast you have there, Donny," said the host. "Is there anything special about him?"

"I was told to say: Shake, Cuddy shake, and see what happened," said Donny, but no sooner had he spoken the words than the pony shook himself, and copper coins came cascading from his chestnut red side, and gold and silver coins showered down from his black and white side. The host and his wife ran about the yard gathering up the coins as they rolled over the cobbles.

"You'd best make him stand on a blanket when you tell him to shake," said the host's wife, red in the face and puffing from running and bending to pick up the treasure. "Then it will all fall in one place!"

"Aye, I'll remember," said Donny. The host and his wife led the pony into the stable, and Donny went to his bed.

But in the morning, the pony that Donny led away was the right colours, but the wrong pony, for the host and his wife had been busy in the night with chalk and soot, to colour their chestnut pony like Donny's.

When Donny arrived, the Factor was paying his visit, and threatening Donny's mother with having to leave the wee house where they had worked so hard to make a living.

"I tellt ye half a crown the last time Missis," the Factor was saying. "And it's gone up to five shillings! Five shillings more on the rent. Times are hard for everyone, ye know."

"And where will I find five more shillings? Ah, you're a hard man and no heart in you at all!" Mammy said. And up rolled Donny and his wee pony.

"Don't worry, Mammy," he said. "Just get a blanket, and watch this!"

The Factor watched as Donny led the pony on to a blanket that his mother had fetched from the house. Mammy and the princess watched, too, in a mixture of hope and misery.

"Shake, Cuddy, shake!" Donny commanded, but of course, nothing happened. Donny tried again, and, sure enough, something fell on to the blanket, but it wasn't gold, silver and copper coins, though it's useful enough for spreading on the garden. The Factor was highly amused, which made Mammy's despair turn to wrath. She chased the Factor from the door, but when he was a safe distance up the road, he turned and shouted: "By the end of the week, Missis, or it's out ye all go, and all your old sticks of furniture!"

Mammy was still cross enough to say to Donny: "Get away up the road back to the House of the Wind, and tell him I don't think much of his reparations!"

Sadly, Donny threw the ball of yarn out before him a third time, and made his way over the fields and hills and running streams.

"It's a pity," said the princess. "He's a good-looking lad with a good heart. If only he was a bit brighter!"

"He was bright enough once," said Mammy, "but he ran foul of the Good Folk on their Dancing Day. He's been the way you see him ever since."

She sighed, and they went back into the house.

Donny arrived once again at the Half-Way House, where once again, he was greeted with smiles and given a bed for the night. The next day, however, as he made his way up the mountain, he met a beautiful lady, all in green, mounted on a snow-white horse.

"Greetings to you, Donny the widow's son," said the lady. "I don't think you remember me, do you?"

"Oh, yes! Yes, I do!" cried Donny: "The Fairies' Dancing Day! You were very cross with me that day!"

"I said that if you should visit the House of the Wind three times, you would have your light restored. And do you remember what else I said to you that day?" she asked, and crooned the song that she had sung to him:

"Thrice to the House of the Wind, thrice,
Three the gifts from the Wind's Dwelling.
Twice the cheating half-way, twice,
But all fair at the final telling."

With that, she rode on her way.

Donny made his way up to the windy summit where the door stood, and again he put his hand over the hole in the heart of the door. Again, the great voice filled all the air round about him.

"WHO'S THAT STOPPING MY BREATH?"

"It's Donny the poor widow's son, come seeking reparation for the hay that was lost!"

"A THIRD TIME YOU COME TO ME, MORTAL? ARE MY GIFTS NOT ENOUGH?"

"Aye, well, see," Donny began, "the quern stone worked fine at the Half-Way House, but it didnae work at all when I got it home. And the wee pony gave off a lot of gold and silver and copper coins at the Half-Way House, but see when we got home, he did nothing!"

"I SHALL GIVE YOU A THIRD GIFT, DONNY THE WIDOW'S SON. SEE THAT YOU USE IT WISELY."

The door swung open, and there on the threshold lay a great long whang of leather and a stick.

"What do I do with these?" Donny asked as he picked them up.

"SAY THE WORDS: BIND THONG, STRIKE STICK. THEY WILL OBEY YOU. HOW YOU USE THEM IS UP TO YOU. FAREWELL. I SHALL MAKE NO MORE REPARATIONS!"

As Donny set off, he felt something changing within his soul. No longer was he slow of thinking, but all his old quickness of mind was coming back to him. He felt, in a word, brighter.

When he arrived at the Half-Way House, he was greeted with all the customary welcome that he had received before.

"Did you go to the House of the Wind, Donny?" asked the host's wife.

"I did."

"And did you get anything there?" asked the host.

"I did."

"And was it a quern stone that grinds all by itself?"

"It was not."

"And was it a pony that shakes gold and silver and copper coins out of its coat?"

"It was not."

"What did you get then, Donny?"

"I got this," said Donny, and showed them the leather thong and the stick. The host and his wife scratched their heads at this.

"But what is the use of these things, Donny?" the host asked.

"Oh," said Donny, much wiser in their ways now. "I'll show you!"

He spoke the words: "Bind thong, strike stick!" And the thong bound the host and his wife together fast, face to face, while the stick attended vigorously to their hinder parts, giving them both a hearty whacking.

"Oh! Oh! Oh!" they cried. "Make it stop, Donny!"

"I will, when you give me back my quern stone and my pony,"

said Donny. Ruefully rubbing their sore and tender backsides, the host and his wife restored to Donny his treasures from the House of the Wind, and Donny went on his way, riding his pony and carrying the magic quern stone; the thong wrapped round his waist, and the stick thrust into his belt like a sword.

When he arrived, the Factor was at the door again, demanding that Mammy and the princess quit the premises at once. Two burly, black-whiskered men were ready to help with the eviction.

"Ah," said the Factor: "The return of the half-witted son! Come on, you great useless lout! Help your mother clear your old lumber out of this!"

"Oh, but wait a bit," said Donny, and the way he said it made Mammy look at him with a touch of hope dawning in her eyes, and the princess looked at him in quite a different way, too; more admiring than she used to.

"Well, what is it? We haven't all day," said the Factor. Donny put down the quern stone, and said: "Mammy, just fetch out the last bag of corn, would you?"

"Oh no, not again, Donny," said Mammy, but Donny had a new way about him, and she went and fetched it.

"Now," said Donny. "Grind, Quern, grind!"

With a great flash, all the corn lay in the sack, ground into fine flour.

"Well now," said the Factor, rubbing his chin, thoughtfully, "I'd better take that thing into custody. It's not canny at all."

"You will not!" Mammy protested, but Donny said, "Wait a moment, Mammy. Just fetch out a blanket, will you?"

Mammy did so, and Donny led the pony on to the blanket.

"Shake, Cuddy, shake!" he commanded, and the pony shook his coat, and copper coins showered down from his chestnut side, and gold and silver from his black and white side, piling up on the blanket in shining heaps.

"Right, well," said the Factor, "I'll just take the horse, and we'll say no more about the rent." He went to take the pony's bridle, but Mammy put herself squarely in the way.

"You'll leave that pony alone!" she said.

The Factor called his men to help, but once again, Donny spoke up.

"There's another thing I have here," he said, and unwound the thong from his waist, and drew the stick from his belt.

"And what's that?" the Factor demanded, his eyes full of greed.

"I'll show you," said Donny, and spoke the words: "Bind thong, strike stick!"

At once, the Factor and his bully-boys were all bound together while the stick beat a lively tattoo on their rear quarters. Soon all three were begging for mercy.

"What's that?" said Donny, "I can't quite hear you."

The stick worked even harder, and the Factor's squeals were the loudest of the three.

"Did you say that you'd run away and leave us alone for ever?" Donny said.

"Yes! Yes! Anything!" the Factor yelled. Donny called off his magical servants the thong and the stick, and the bully-boys ran away up the road with all haste, while the Factor, who seemed to have got the worst of the drubbing, hobbled lamely away in the other direction.

Just at that moment, a coach drew up, and a man all in rich apparel climbed out.

"It's the Shanacal!" said the princess.

"It is indeed, Your Highness," said the Shanacal, "And I bring a message from your father the King of Erin. He wishes you and your husband to come back to his castle, as he misses you more than he can say."

"Can Mammy come too?" asked Donny, "and my pony?"

"I see no objection," said the Shanacal, "though perhaps you may all wish to change into clothing more suited to the royal palace."

"But I've nothing of that class of clothes at all!" said Mammy.

"We'll buy something on the way," said Donny, "for we're rich as any king now!"

Sure enough, thanks to the pony, they were never short of riches.

Donny's last act before leaving was to give the magic quern stone to the Spaewife. After that, they set off for the green shores of Erin, where they all lived happily to the end of their days.

"It was a good thing for Donny and his mother that the Spaewife happened by at the right moment," said the Dark Stranger.

"It was all of that," said Shifty, "and such people are rare, and the training is hard and dangerous."

"So you think they train?" the Dark Stranger asked. "They aren't born with the gift?"

"Some are born with the gift, right enough," said Shifty, "but others, like Michael Scott, had to learn his lessons to become the mighty warlock of Aikwood."

"Such lessons are not learned in school," said the Dark Stranger.

"No, indeed," said Shifty, "and I'll tell you where Michael Scott gained his education, and his adventures that followed."

Michael Scott's Graduation

Michael Scott was from the Border country, where he went to school, and was a very able scholar. He was also at the University at Durham among the English, Paris in France and Bologna in Italy, but the place where he learned his magical skills was in a tall, round tower in the depths of the Ettrick Forest. It's said that only those who come seeking the place can find it, and not always then; but Michael found the tower easily enough.

The Rector of the school was Dòmhnull Dubh, Black Donald himself, for that is the name we give to Auld Clootie, or Auld Nick; or, as some folk whisper it: the devil. He welcomed his students gladly. There, they learned all the warlock's arts, such as healing sick animals and men; casting horoscopes; reading the future; reading the language of the elements, wind, water, earth and fire; casting spells to help — or harm: and many others besides.

One day, Auld Nick the Rector, called all his students together.

"Now, my bonny boys," he said: "You are all progressing well in your studies, and I have high hopes of you. It will not be long before you all graduate from our academy. Remember always to charge highly for your services, and curse and blast those who cheat you, or try to wheedle you into accepting a lower fee.

"On the Day of Graduation, you will all assemble in the Great Hall, and I shall call you up one by one to receive your diplomas from my own hand. When you take your diploma, you will return to your seat at once. When each man has received his diploma, you are free to go, but ... The last one to reach the door must remain here with me to be my servant in the Hot Place — for ever!"

This news ran round the students like a cold flame. Each man wanted to gain power in the world through what he had learned, but none of them wanted to remain behind as a servant of Auld Hornie! Some hit upon the plan of stealing away on the night before the graduation ceremony, but Michael Scott was wiser than these. While others decided to depend on their brute strength to get them through the door, and others thought up schemes to escape before the fatal moment, Michael studied the rising of the sun, the position of the door, and the way the shadows fall. At last, he was satisfied with his researches, and got on with his studies calmly and without fear.

At last, the night before the graduation arrived. Those that sought to escape found that, no matter what they did, whether trying the door, or climbing out of the windows, or even getting out into the precincts of the tower (which a couple of them managed to do) they all found themselves, sooner or later, lying in their cots in the dormitory, and all their efforts no more than dreams. Michael, all the while, slept like a baby.

The next day, the students all gathered in the Great Hall, and the list of names was read out, and each man went up to collect his diploma. The anxiety grew greater and greater as the list grew shorter and shorter. Finally, the last name was read out, and the last man went up to collect his vellum parchment on which the diploma was written out.

"Well done my bonny boys all," the Rector said, "and now, you are all …" He paused for a few fateful seconds, the light glinting in his eye, and at last cried, "dismissed!"

There was a terrible scramble for the door, and an ugly stramash as they kicked and fought and punched to get away, and avoid being a servant in the hot and shadowy lands for ever. Michael Scott, however, calmly waited until the doorway was at last clear, and sauntered carelessly towards it.

"I believe you're the last one out, Michael Scott!" said Dòmhnull Dubh, the king of the Hot Place.

"Oh, d'ye think so?" said Michael, as he stood in the doorway. And, pointing at his shadow that fell exactly into the hall behind him, Michael said: "I think there's yer mannie!"

For Michael had studied the rising and setting of the sun, and he knew that on the Day of Graduation, a man's shadow would fall across the floor at the doorway. And from that day onward, Michael Scott never cast a shadow, even in brightest sunlight, for his shadow was the devil's servant for ever.

"But you must be well acquainted with the Lord of the Land of Heat and Shadows," said Shifty. "You are at his service, are you not?"

"Acquainted with him, yes, I am," said the Dark Stranger, "but he is not my master. I have commissions that lead me along the bright road, too."

"It would be a clever man indeed who knows the different roads that you travel," said Shifty, thoughtfully.

"Cleverness solves a lot of a person's difficulties," said the Dark Stranger. "But I know well that it can get a person into difficulties, too. Witness your clever self, my Shifty Lad!"

"Yes," said Shifty. "I think my case is as hard as that of the Welsh farmer that I once heard about. He was a man who thought himself clever, right enough."

"How did his cleverness serve him?" the Dark Stranger asked.

"The way I heard it was like this," said Shifty, and this was the next tale he told.

The Cow on the Roof

Ianto Prytherch was a very lucky man. He had married a
beautiful girl called Myfanwy Price, and they had a fine baby
and a piece of good land.

One day, Ianto came home from the field worn out with
working.

"Come in and sit down, cariad," said Myfanwy, "I'll get
your dinner on the table now."

"It's all right for you," he told Myfanwy, "all you have to do
is potter around here at home. Nothing but the baby and one
or two bits of pieces of work like washing up. Meanwhile, I'm
breaking my back out there among the turnips."

"I'd change places with you tomorrow, if you think like
that," she replied, "But I reckon you'd find it harder than you
think, Ianto bach!"

This got under Ianto's collar, and he raised his voice to his wife.

"Harder than I think? Harder than I think, woman? By
damn, I tell you, I'll swop places with you tomorrow, and
then we'll see! Harder than I think! Tchah!"

Well, now Myfanwy was getting a bit cross, too, and she
said: "All right, Ianto Prytherch! Tomorrow morning, I'll go
out into the field, and you can stay at home here and look
after the baby and see to the house, and we'll see who gets the
best of the bargain!"

And so the bargain was struck. The next day, Myfanwy would
go out into the field, and Ianto would remain in the house and
look after the baby, and see to all the chores. They exchanged
never a word more that evening, but ate their dinners in silence.

Next morning, Myfanwy pulled on her thickest, stoutest boots
and took a warm coat, and set off for the field. Ianto allowed

himself another hour in bed, looking forward to a pleasant, easy day.

"I'll show her," he said to himself, chuckling: "I'll show her!"

Now, there was the baby to take care of, the porage to make, the pig to be fed, and an eye was to be kept on the cow, that she didn't wander off into the field next door and eat the wheat. The cow was the most difficult, for the fence needed mended, and she was liable to go off on to the neighbour's land and cause damage, if Ianto wasn't careful.

Then he had a clever idea. The house lay just below the field, and the roof was a turf roof, and all grass. If Ianto could get the cow on to the roof, he would know where she was, and he would get the grass, that was growing too long, down to a good length by letting the cow eat it. There was clever, now, he thought. Carefully, he led the cow to the edge of the field above the house, and he gave her rump a kick that made her jump on to the roof, where she started happily grazing.

One thing bothered Ianto, though. The roof was sloping, and he was afraid that she might fall off, and he would know nothing about it, until it was too late. But now he had another clever idea. He fetched a length of rope and tied one end round the cow's neck. Here was the clever part: he dropped the other end down the chimney, and once inside the house, he tied this other end round his leg. Then he would know if the cow was somewhere that she shouldn't be. He rubbed his hands thinking about his cleverness, and began to stir the porage.

The baby started crying. Now, Ianto didn't know much about babies, and didn't know that this baby wanted his nappy changed. He just rocked the baby's cradle as he stirred the porage, but baby wasn't soothed by the rocking at all. He just cried the louder, and Ianto rocked harder.

Now the pig, who lived in the sty across the yard, hadn't yet been fed, and he was very cross about that. He snorted and snuffled and banged himself against the sty door.

"I'll deal with you in a minute," Ianto shouted, but the pig was not satisfied with that, and snorted and snuffled and banged all the louder. Meanwhile, the baby was crying with wanting to be changed, and with Ianto rocking him about so roughly, and Ianto was still stirring the porage with the other hand.

Now a pig isn't necessarily the most patient of animals, and he was now battering the sty door with all his might, snuffling and snorting angrily. All of a sudden, the sty door burst open with the battering, and the pig came galloping across the yard and right into the kitchen! He ran round the kitchen, knocking over the churn full of buttermilk, and the bucket full of pig swill. Ianto looked at the terrible mess on the floor, all swimming in pigswill and buttermilk, and in a rage, he dropped the spoon into the porage, left the baby's cradle swinging all by itself, with the baby yelling his loudest, and he fetched his hammer, and gave the pig an almighty wallop on the head, and laid the poor beast out cold.

Just then, the cow fell off the roof.

Now, it was clever of Ianto, right enough, to make sure by tying the rope round his leg that he would know if the cow went somewhere that she shouldn't. Where his cleverness let him down, though, was in not realising that the cow was much heavier than he was, and now she had fallen off the roof, and her weight pulled Ianto, on the other end of the rope, up the chimney. But the chimney was narrow, and Ianto was jammed, upside down.

Round about mid-morning, Myfanwy started back to the house for her eleven o' clock cup of tea, and to see how Ianto was getting on. She wasn't far away when she heard the baby crying, so she hurried over the field, and saw a strange sight: the cow dangling by a rope at the side of the house, and not looking at all pleased about the situation. She took a sharp knife and cut the rope, and led the cow into the byre to recover. Then she went into the house.

What a sight met her eyes there! Across the doorway was a pig, apparently fast asleep. The floor was awash with buttermilk, pigswill and soot, the baby was yelling lustily with rage and discomfort, and there was no sign of Ianto.

Myfanwy changed the baby's nappy and soothed him to sleep. She woke up the pig, and led him back to the sty, and started to get to work cleaning up the kitchen floor, and then she saw Ianto. He was upside down in the fireplace, with his legs up the chimney and his head stuck in the porage pot.

She helped him out, helped him to clean off the porage and brush off the soot, and together they cleaned up the mess in the kitchen. Ianto didn't have much to say for himself, and hardly dared to catch Myfanwy's eye, for fear that she would either burst out raging at him, or laugh at him, which would be worse, for you can meet rage with rage, but laughter is harder to face.

Wisely, Myfanwy said nothing about it. And that night, as they lay in bed in the darkness, Myfanwy said lightly: "So will you go to work in the field tomorrow, then?"

"Aye," said Ianto, "I think probably it's best, on the whole. After all, it's not a woman's work, is it now."

That was when Myfanwy began to laugh, and Ianto didn't feel quite so clever after all. But he never ever complained about working out in the field again.

"So the woman showed herself to be the wiser in the end," said the Dark Stranger.

"True, but some women need the help that the spirits in nature can give them," said Shifty. "Such as the woman who lived in the lee of Slievenamon."

"How was that?" asked the Dark One, full of curiosity.

The Horned Women

There was a house that lay in the shadow of the Mountain of the Women, which is called Slievenamon in Erin. The goodwife of this house was well-to-do, and had three children and seven servants.

She sat up one night, carding wool for spinning, when a great knock came at the door, and a voice cried: "Open! Open!"

"Who is it?" asked the woman of the house, and the reply came: "I am the witch of one horn!"

The woman could not quite believe what she heard, and thought that a neighbour had come wanting help. She opened the door, and in rushed a woman with wool-carders in her hands, and a horn growing in the centre of her forehead. She sat by the fire, and began carding wool, as though in a great hurry. The woman of the house found that she could not utter a sound, for the horned woman held her spellbound.

At last the horned woman cried: "Where are the women? Why do they delay? They take too long!"

Just then, there came a knock at the door again, and a voice, crying: "Open, open!"

Unable to help herself, the woman of the house went and opened the door, and in came a second witch, with two horns on her head. She carried in her hands a spinning wheel.

"Make way for me," she said. "I am the witch of the two horns."

She sat at the fire beside the first, and began spinning wool with great speed, and there was nothing the woman of the house could say or do in the presence of these strange creatures. She sat as if bewitched, which indeed she was.

As the night wore on, there came more knocking, and even more, until at last, twelve women sat at the fire, all with horns on their heads to the number of twelve, carding, spinning and weaving wool, and singing together strange, ancient songs, but the woman of the house was helpless in their power, and reduced to being their servant in all they demanded of her. All she could do was watch, as ten of the strange women sat spinning; one sat carding wool, and one weaving it.

Then one of the horned women ordered her to rise and fetch water to bake a cake. She rose to do as she was commanded, but could find no bowl or vessel in which to fetch the water.

"Take a sieve and fetch the water in it," another of the weird sisters ordered. The woman of the house, though she feared mightily for the children asleep in the house, could do no other than to take a sieve and went to the well, but the water ran through it. The poor woman's tears flowed for misery, and she sat down by the well and wept.

From the well, a voice spoke to her, saying: "Take moss and clay and mix them together, and line the bottom of the sieve."

The woman did so, and soon had her sieve full of good water. She washed her tear-stained face in the sieve full of well water, and the spell on her was broken.

"Take the water to the house," said the voice, "But when you come to the north corner of the house, cry out in a loud voice three times: 'The Mountain of the Fenian women, and the sky above it is all on fire!'"

The woman went to the north corner of the house, and cried out as the voice had advised her. At once, the twelve horned women gave a great shriek, and they ran out of the house, crying and keening, running to Slievenamon, which they called their home.

Inside the house, the twelve women had not waited for the water to bake their cake, but had taken blood from each of the sleeping children and servants in the house as they lay in their beds, and now they lay pale and almost lifeless.

The voice of the spirit of the well told the woman what she had to do. She was to take the water with which she washed the children's feet, and sprinkle it across the threshold at the door, for it is well-known that the feet-water has a power of its own.

Then, the spirit of the well told her to take the cake and break it, and place a piece of it in the mouths of each of the sleeping children and servants. This she did, and the colour of life came back to their cheeks and lips.

"Now take the cloth that the weaver-woman has woven," said the voice, "And place it half in and half out of the chest, and relock the padlock."

This the woman did, and finally, she placed the great heavy beam across the door, driving it hard into the hasps in the door jambs, so that none could enter. Then, she sat down to wait.

It was not long before the witches came hurrying back, full of fury, and intent on vengeance. When they found that they could not open the door, they ran round the house, muttering together and looking for a way in. The woman of the house heard their skirts rustling outside, and saw their terrible faces close up at the fast-shut windows. Some tried the chimney, but the woman built up the fire, and they could not come in that way.

"Open! Open feet-water!" they cried, but a voice came from the ground at the threshold, saying: "Alas, I cannot, for I am scattered over the ground, and my path is all down to the lough."

"Open! Open wood and beam," cried the horned women.

"I am fixed fast in the door jambs, and can do nothing," came a voice from the door beam.

"Open! Open cloth on the loom!" cried the women.

"Alas, I am neither in nor out of the locked chest, and can do nothing," came another voice.

"Open, open cake made and mixed and mingled with the blood of the children!" screamed the women.

"Alas, I am all broken, and I lie on the lips of the sleeping children and servants," came a voice from the bedroom.

Then the witches all gave a great cry of rage, and streaked away back to the mountain, uttering curses on the spirit of the well. But the woman was left in peace, and a cloak that fell from the shoulders of one of the horned women was kept in the woman's family for many generations thereafter, for five hundred years.

"It was wise of the woman to listen to the voice of the spirit of the well," said the Stranger.

"Och, there are many tales about the wisdom of women," said Shifty: "I'll tell you now about Lord Edgar's daughter and the King of Lochlann."

"That tale must wait," said the Dark Stranger, "for we must be on our way."

"How are we to travel? Do you have a wondrous horse, like Michael Scott's?" asked Shifty.

"A wondrous horse?" asked the dark one.

"Why, yes," Shifty replied, and told the tale of Michael Scott's wonderful horse.

Michael Scott's Horse

There was a time when the folk of Scotland were vexed to know how to tell the date of Easter. In the old days, the date had been fixed, like Michaelmas, or Hogmanay, and there was no question about it. But now times had changed, and the date of Easter was no longer fixed. This was a difficulty, for the people had no way of knowing when Shrove Tuesday was going to fall, for Shrove Tuesday comes before Lent, and Lent comes before Easter; but if you don't know when Easter is, you don't know when Shrove Tuesday will fall, and that was hard for the folk not knowing when to make their Shrove Tuesday pancakes, and to begin their fasting for Lent.

There was one person who could help them, and this was Michael Scott, so a group of important bodies, such as the Laird and the Provost, went to Michael Scott to ask him if he could help them in this hard case.

Michael readily agreed. "I shall go to the Pope in Rome himself, and ask him," he promised.

"But how will you travel?" they asked, worried that there would not be time enough for Michael to travel to Rome and back in time for Shrove Tuesday.

Travelling was no worry to Michael at all, especially travelling at great speed, for what he had learned at the Devil's round tower in Aikwood, and what he had learned from the witches' broth — another tale that I'll tell you another time — had given him the power to command demons from the Hot Place to do his bidding.

Now there was one unruly demon that Michael had mastered, and turned into the likeness of a horse, a great black beast with flashing red eyes, and this creature could fly through the air at great speed. Michael went to his stable and saddled and bridled his terrible steed, and none but he could ride him, and away with him up into the air towards Rome.

This demon could never understand how Michael had gained mastery of him, and he turned to him in flight and said: "How do you have this power over me, Michael Scott?" But Michael just laughed and cried: "Mount higher, Devil!" And in a matter of minutes, they arrived in Rome.

Michael tethered his steed at a wayside cross, where it could do nothing but lie still until Michael came for it again, and went to seek audience with the Pope.

"Ah! Michael Scott!" said His Holiness. "What brings you here? Have you changed your mind about becoming the Bishop of Cashel?"

"Indeed no, I havena," replied Michael.

"Then are you seeking forgiveness for translating unholy foreign books from infidel tongues into Latin?" demanded the Pope, for this was a sore point between them.

"Indeed no, I seek no forgiveness for that," Michael answered.

"Then have you come asking my pardon for poisoning the mind of the German Emperor against me?" the Pope asked, for he believed that Michael had done that when the German Emperor was just a boy at his lessons, and Michael his teacher.

"The German Emperor made up his own mind about you, with no help from me," said Michael.

"Then, you hard and stubborn man, explain to me the reason for your visit," the Pope said.

"It is this, Your Holiness," said Michael: "My folk at home in Scotland are toiling to know when to make ready to keep Lent a holy time, in readiness to keep the great holiday of Easter. And they canna do this until they know when Easter is to be. It would be a great service to those poor suffering folk if they knew how to organize their lives fittingly."

"Very well," replied the Pope, "For their sake and not for yours, I shall tell you that Easter Sunday shall fall on the First

Sunday after the first Full Moon after the Spring Equinox. And now, shall I tell you why this is so?"

"Nae need," said Michael, and bowing quickly, he hurried from the Pope's presence to where his black demon horse stood tethered by the wayside cross.

As he approached it, two peasants came running towards him, crying: "Master! Master! Don't go near that horse! One of our men tried to mount him, and he turned and breathed fire at him, and burned his hand full sore!"

"Your friend maybe has something to learn about such creatures," said Michael, and leaped gaily on to his horse's back. The peasants stood amazed and dumbfounded as Michael cried: "Home, Devil!" and flew away into the air.

"How is it that you have this mastery over me?" the demon horse whinnied, as they mounted among the clouds. Again, Michael just laughed, and cried: "Mount higher, Devil!"

When they had arrived back in Scotland, Michael at once went to the Laird and the Provost, and told them that Easter Sunday would fall on the first Sunday after the first full Moon after the Spring Equinox, and they went away and made their calculations, and determined which day that would be, and therefore which day Shrove Tuesday would be, and it has been thus ever since.

"No such beast have I," said the Dark Stranger, "nor need of one. Make ready, my Shifty Lad!"

"Indeed I will," said Shifty, "Though the strangest beast I ever heard of was the cat in the change-house, or inn on the road to Tobermory. This cat was lying quite still and cosy by the fire, when a man came into the change-house and demanded a drink of good whisky, for he could not get over what he had just seen. They asked him what it was, but he had to finish his drink and take another before he could tell them. He had been making his way through Argyll, when he came upon a solemn procession of cats on the road, carrying a funeral casket, all draped with fine cloth of the richest sort. He followed them into a clearing in the wood, and there, they dug a hole, and put the casket in, and spoke words over the grave which must have been all in Irish, for the man could understand little of their Gaelic, other than the word Righ, which they mentioned many times, so it was some sort of king that was being buried. Well, when the cat by the fire heard this, he sat up, and spoke like any Christian, saying, 'Why, the traitors! The traitors! But now I am King of the Cats!' And away he flew up the chimney. All of them needed a strong drink of good whisky after that! I imagine Yves the Breton haberdasher needed a good reviver, too, after his journey home from market."

And this was the tale he told next.

The Miser's Ghost

The people of Brittany in France are very close kin with the people of Cornwall and Wales, and they share their tales and songs. One tale they tell is of a man called Yves, who was a haberdasher by trade, and would travel to the markets all over Brittany, setting up his stall to sell needles and threads of all colours, scissors and other tools of the trades of tailor or seamstress.

One night, a night of bright moonlight, he was making his way home from the market in a town called Quimper, when he came upon a graveyard. This graveyard was well known to Yves, and in daylight, he would often take a short cut through it. At night, he was less willing to do so, but it was still a long way to go home, and every little helps, as they say. So he crossed the graveyard.

As he did so, a figure seemed to rise and go before him. Yves looked, and saw that it was a figure he well knew by his walk and shape. It was old Serre-sou, the miser. Any other time, this would have been of no surprise to Yves, for the old man liked to sit in the graveyard. Now, however, it was a shock, for old Serre-sou had been dead for a fortnight.

The figure of the old man shuffled along before him, never turning his face to Yves, but Yves knew that if he was not settled in his grave, there must be something troubling him, and his way to Paradise was barred for some reason.

Yves was filled with compassion for the poor soul, and put down his heavy pack. He called out to him, "Maître Serre-sou! Maître Serre-sou! Is there anything I can do for you?"

The figure made no sign of having heard him, and vanished into the shadows. Yves shouldered his heavy pack again, and continued on his way, his heart heavy on behalf of the poor miser, whose spirit could find no rest. Indeed, Yves had heard that the old miser's last act on his death-bed was to reach towards his chest, where he kept his riches. The priest, who was visiting him in his last hours begged him not to exert himself too much, but the effort was too much for the old man, and he expired in that moment.

The priest had said, to anyone who cared to listen, that old Serre-sou was trying to give his worldly goods to the Church in expiation for a life of greed and avarice, but no-one believed it of the old miser.

The road was broad, and clear in the moonlight as Yves made his way homewards, and there again, up ahead of him, appeared the figure of the miser, shuffling along sadly.

"Maître Serre-sou, Maître Serre-sou! Please, if I can do anything for you, just tell me, or make me a sign."

Still there was no response from the hunched and shuffling figure, who walked on ahead of Yves, turned the corner of the road, and was no more to be seen. Yves felt sad at heart that there was nothing that he could do to help the restless spirit, but walked on along the moonlit road.

The road turned, and soon there was a crossroads before him. In France, there is hardly a crossroads that does not have its wayside cross for poor travellers to make their prayers and devotions. This crossroads was no exception, but opposite the cross was an old, dry well. The figure of the miser appeared beside the well, and, though still not turning to look at Yves, raised one finger, as though asking him to wait.

As Yves watched, the old man's spirit climbed into the well, and Yves heard footsteps, as of someone going down a spiral staircase into a deep cellar. Yves hurried to the cross, and knelt before it, saying prayers for the old miser's soul.

As he prayed, he could hear a sound, deep underground, as of great sacks full of money being dragged from under the well to beneath the cross, far under the place where he knelt. Yves closed his eyes tightly, and prayed fervently on behalf of old Serre-sou.

Then, as he opened his eyes, looking up, he saw a shooting star! At that, he felt a great lightness in his heart, for that is the sign that another soul had gained entry to Paradise. He shouldered his pack, and went gladly on his way.

"Will there be any to pray in like manner for you, my Shifty Lad?" the Hooded Stranger asked, with a cold curling smile at the corner of his mouth.

"I can only hope so," said Shifty, his mind straying to the folk who had suffered because of his dealings: the shepherd, the Black Rogue and his wife, the carpenter — not forgetting his own mother, too. And then there was the princess. How he longed to see her again!

"But here!" he cried, "I promised to tell you about Lord Edgar's Daughter and the King of Lochlann!"

Lord Edgar's Daughter and the King of Lochlann

The Land of Lochlann is what we would call Norway these days, but Lochlann it was to the folk of Scotland and Erin in the days when the Long Ships were on the sea. Sometimes they were welcome, and sometimes they were met with fear and dread, for the men of Lochlann were terrible fierce warriors.

Many of them settled in Scotland and Erin, and, they tell me, in England, too, and when things were friendly between us and Lochlann, all went well. And it was in a friendly time that the King of Lochlann came to Scotland seeking a bride.

He was met and welcomed by Lord Edgar, a great Scottish noble, who had invited all the beautiful daughters of Scottish noblemen to his castle, so that the King of Lochlann could select a bride from among them, for well he knew that Scottish girls are among the most beautiful in the world, but they are also hardy, hard-working and sensible, and these were qualities that the Lochlann king wanted in a wife.

Now, Lord Edgar had a daughter himself, and a fair and lovely girl she was, too, who enjoyed no better companionship than that of her pet greyhound. The fellowship of fine ladies was not for her, neither were the manners and fashions of the royal household of any interest to her.

She asked her father if she could take her place among the ladies gathered in the hall, but her father angrily refused.

"You are getting ideas above your station, lassie!" he thundered.

"I am as nobly born as any of these," she protested, "and as good as any of them!"

"Indeed and you are," said Lord Edgar, "but see now! How would it look if I invited all of the fine ladies of Scotland to my house, and the King of Lochlann chose you? It would look bad! People would accuse me of pride and boastfulness. They would think that I had invited the ladies here just to shame them! No no, it would never do, lassie, it would never do!"

"But the King of Lochlann will make his own choice, will he not?"

"He will."

"So could I not take my chances with all the other lassies?"

"I have told you," said Lord Edgar, "and I shall not tell you again! You are not to enter into the hall!"

"May I watch from the door, then?"

"Aye, so far you may come. But no farther!"

And so it was that all the fine ladies of Scottish noble houses arrived at Lord Edgar's castle, and some of them came in velvet red, and some in velvet pale, yet no place among them for Lord Edgar's daughter, the fairest of them all. She stood at the doorway, watching all the ladies in their finery, and looking at the King of Lochlann, tall and handsome, with his long fair hair and his piercing gaze, standing before the fire and considering all the ladies who hoped to become his queen.

At last, he spoke, and this is what he said:

"Ladies, I thank you all for coming. All of you are worthy to be queens, and no doubt many of you are queens to come. If it were a matter of beauty, I should be hard pressed to make a choice. But I must have a wife of good sense and a quick and witty mind. Therefore, I issue a challenge to you all. If you wish to be my wife, and the Queen of Lochlann, you should come to my boat in the dawn, not dressed, but not naked; nether feasting nor fasting; neither alone, nor bearing company. These are my conditions. Is there anyone here who can fulfil all of them?"

The ladies all looked at each other in surprise and disappointment. None of them expected to have to satisfy such conditions, and how could they be satisfied? How could one be neither dressed nor naked? How can one be neither feasting not fasting? Either you have your breakfast, or you do not. There is surely nothing in between? And how could one be neither alone, nor bearing any company? It was absurd, and a trick, and impossible! Some grew angry and others just looked puzzled, while others laughed in good humour. Others began to weep with disappointment.

But then a voice came from the doorway.

"I can answer all these conditions!"

Everyone turned to see Lord Edgar's daughter at the threshold. There she stood, no finery about her or rich adornments; only a plain dress and her own beauty.

"Was it you who spoke, young woman?" asked the King.

"It was I indeed," she replied.

"Well, don't stand in the doorway; come into the hall where all can see you," the King commanded.

"Ah, but my father has forbidden me to come into the hall," said the young woman, glancing at her father as she spoke.

"He will allow you if I request it," said the King, looking at Lord Edgar. The girl's father nodded his assent, and turned away to hide his feelings. The young woman walked into the hall, and all the ladies looked at her as she passed, some looking in curiosity, others with contempt at her plain dress, others with envy at her beauty.

At last she stood before the King of Lochlann, looking him in the eye.

"So you say that you can fulfil my conditions?" said the King.

"I do," she said. There was a sensation among the ladies. How could this young woman, this mere girl, know how to meet the conditions set by the King?

"Then I shall await you at my boat at dawn tomorrow morning," said the King. The ladies now began to leave, some in high dudgeon, some in disappointment, some wondering how Lord Edgar's daughter would manage so impossible a task.

Lord Edgar was angry with his daughter, and told her plainly to expect no dowry from him.

"I ask nothing from you, father," she said, "but an old fishing net and an onion."

"Take them and go," her father said.

In the cold dawn light of the next morning, the King of Lochlann waited with one foot on the gunwale of his longship, to see whether Lord Edgar's daughter would indeed be able to come to him neither clothed, nor naked, neither feasting nor fasting, and neither alone nor bearing no company.

Then, through the mist, he saw a figure approaching the quay. It was indeed Lord Edgar's daughter.

"And have you fulfilled my wishes?" he called to her through the mist of the coming day.

"I have," she replied.

"So you are neither naked nor dressed?"

"See for yourself. I am wrapped in nothing but this fishing net."

"Good. That was the first condition. Now, are you neither feasting nor fasting?"

The girl took the onion that she was holding in her right hand, and bit into it.

"See," she said, "I neither feast nor fast."

The King of Lochlann laughed aloud, and the laughter echoed through the dawn light.

"Very good! But what about the third condition? You were to come bearing no company, but not alone."

The girl turned and whistled two sharp, shrill notes, and her greyhound came faithfully trotting up to stand beside her.

"See," she said, "I bear no human company, but I am not alone."

"Good again," said the King. "Now come aboard, my lassie, and we shall exchange your fishnet for the finest dresses, and that onion for the best food, and besides your greyhound, you shall have my company. Does that please you?"

"It pleases me fine," she replied, and they set sail for the land of Lochlann, where they lived happily until the end of their days.

"So you see," said Shifty, "she was a clever lassie as well as beautiful."

"Aye," said the Dark Stranger, "it is often the way that the womenfolk are wiser than the men."

"Just so," agreed Shifty, "like the wife of the farmer in Wales who met an imp one day. The way it happened was like this ..."

The Farmer and the Imp *

There was a poor Welsh farmer who was at his wits' end. His crops wouldn't grow, his beasts wouldn't thrive, and he was in debt to such an extent that he knew he could never pay it all off. In this sad and desperate condition, he wandered away into the woods near his house, half thinking about whether it would be better to hang himself up from a tree, or just to throw himself into a pond and make an end of it all that way.

Well, as often happens in such a case, who should spring up from behind a bush, but an imp, a wicked sprite, who laughed at him, and asked why he was in such a miserable state in his soul.

"Ah," said the farmer, "my animals will not thrive, no matter how well I keep and feed them; my crops will not come up in spite of all my care for them, and I owe more money than I can pay off in my lifetime. There's no more I can do. I'm finished, just."

"Perhaps I can help you," said the imp. "I can make your fortunes turn for the better."

"Well," said the farmer, "Don't think I don't appreciate the offer, but I doubt if you can help me."

"Oh, let me try, at least," said the imp with a wicked leer, "and I'll only put one simple condition on the offer."

"One condition?" said the farmer, "and what would that be, now?"

"I shall make your fortunes turn to your advantage," said the imp, "and in return, seven years from this day, I shall return. You must then show me an animal that I have never seen before, and I shall consider our bargain fulfilled."

"What sort of an animal would that be?" asked the farmer, but the imp did not reply. All he said was: "And if you can't show me an animal that I've never seen before, you'll have to come along with me to view the ovens of the Hot Place. Now, is it a bargain?" and he held out his hand to shake.

In a daze, the farmer shook the imp's hand; hot and scaly though it was, and returned to his house wondering whether he had dreamed the whole encounter, or if it was the effect of eating mealy potatoes.

When he got in, his wife told him that there was a letter waiting for him.

"More bills I suppose," said the farmer, opening the letter, "more bills that I can't pay."

But his face changed when he read the letter, for it told him that his rich uncle Huw Pugh had passed away, and left him his farm and all his money in his will.

Now, Huw Pugh's farm was large and thriving, and the money he left was plentiful, and soon the farmer was doing very well. In fact, he grew to be the most prosperous farmer in the district, and grew something of a belly to prove the point. He and his wife had seven fine children, and all went well for them.

But as the years went by, he came to wonder more and more about his meeting in the woods with the imp, and whether it was an infernal hand that was guiding his fortunes and prosperity.

The more he thought about it, the more anxious he became, and all his round belly shrank away with the worry. Meanwhile, the days were adding up towards the seven years that the imp had stipulated.

Now, the farmer's wife had noticed this change in her man, and she began to ask him what he was worrying about.

"Oh, just nothing at all," he would say, "just nothing at all."

Well, this would not do as an answer to a woman such as she was, and she kept asking him and asking him.

"You've been gambling away the profits, is that it?"

"No, no. Not at all," he would reply.

"Well, it must be something," she insisted, "for you're not sleeping. And if you can't sleep, I can't sleep, with you tossing and turning and moaning all night. So come on, boy bach, out with it!"

At last the farmer gave in, and told her all about the meeting in the woods on the day that he thought he would bring a sharp end to all his problems.

"And you see," he explained, "if I am not able show him an animal that he's never seen before, I have to toddle along with him to view the ovens of hell. And hot it is indeed that they are, so they tell me!"

"Well, is that it?" she cried. "Is that all? And here's me worrying about you night after night, and not sleeping! Well, that's easy to fix. When is this fellow due to come back?"

The farmer told her that it was in two days' time.

"Good," says she. "Here's what I want you to do: go to the barn and sweep the floor clean. That's the first thing."

So off the farmer went to sweep the byre floor clean of all dust and stoor and dirt and muck, and a good, thorough job he made of it, too.

"Now," she said, "fill a barrow with pig's muck, and bring it to the byre."

Off the farmer went, having no idea what was in his wife's mind, but trusting that her idea was sound.

"Now," she said, when the barrow full of pig's muck was ready; "Spread the muck over half of the floor. Just half of the floor, mind; I don't want it everywhere!"

The farmer now was beginning to think that she had lost her reason through all the sleepless nights that he had given her, but he did as he was told.

"The next thing," she said, "is to fetch the sacks of feathers that we plucked off the geese and turkeys last Christmas."

Well by this time, the farmer was sure that she had gone daft, and when she told him to spread the feathers from last year's geese and turkeys over the clean half of the byre floor, he was sure of it.

"What next?" he asked, nervously, horrified to think what else she would ask him to do, but she said: "Nothing else. Just wait till he comes now."

Of course the farmer slept not a wink, while his wife slept as sound as a baby. But on the morning when the imp was due to arrive, she got up early and went down to the barn, taking the farmer with her.

She took off her night dress, and rolled over and over and over one way in the pig muck, and then she rolled over and over and over the other way, until she was all covered in it. Now the farmer was certain that she was crazy. But when she rolled over and over and over in the feathers, he began to see what she was up to. Then, they got the children together, and in one great game, the children all covered themselves in pig muck and feathers, too, and what a sight they all were, to be sure.

At last they all stood up, covered in muck and feathers, and completely unrecognizable. She stood in the middle of the byre floor, and danced a merry dance, and the children danced with her.

"Now," she said, "take the children into the woods while he's here."

The farmer laughed and laughed, and, wiping the tears of laughter from his eyes, took the children to hide in the woods before going to meet the imp.

"Ho ho!" cried the imp, leaping up from behind the gatepost as the farmer returned.

"Bore da," said the farmer, politely, which is Welsh for 'Good morning'.

"I think your fortunes are in a better case than when we last met?" asked the imp.

"They are indeed, thank you kindly," the farmer replied.

"And do you remember our bargain?"

"I do," said the farmer. "Would you like to come down to the farm with me?"

"It would be a pleasure," said the imp, greedily, and together they made their way to the farm.

"Now," said the imp, "can you show me an animal that I've never seen before?"

"Well, what about this?" said the farmer, pointing out a fine ram.

"No good. I've seen sheep before," said the imp.

"And this?" the farmer said, showing the imp a goat, chewing a mouthful of feed.

"Oh, I know goats of old," said the imp.

"And no doubt you'll have seen one of these?" the farmer said, pointing out his fine sow.

"I'm well acquainted with pigs," said the imp. "Come now, farmer, you'll have to do better than this!"

"Now here's a fine specimen," said the farmer, showing the imp his sheepdog, but the imp stamped his foot.

"Farmer! Come now! One last chance! And if I can't name it, you'll have to toddle along with me!"

"Very well," said the farmer, and he led the imp to the barn, where his wife was still dancing in the middle of the floor.

The imp's eyes bulged in his head and his mouth hung open in dismay.

"What ... What ...What *is it?*" he gasped.

"I was hoping you'd be able to tell me," said the farmer, "for I've seven more in the woods yonder."

He pointed, and sure enough, there were seven more of these strange creatures, all dancing in and out among the trees.

"But ... But ..." stuttered the imp, and at last, he turned from green to black to red, swelled up and exploded, leaving nothing but a smell of sulphur, smoke and burning behind him, and he never troubled the farmer or his family ever again.

"It can be a hard life, being a farmer, right enough," said the Dark Stranger. "But we must be about our business now. Come on."

"A hard life? Indeed, it is all of that," agreed Shifty. "Particularly when you're bothered with the Good Folk, as we call them. That's what happened to Luran MacDhui, but I'll tell you the tale as I heard it."

The Dark Stranger turned from the edge of the battlements to listen.

Luran and the Fairy Hill

There never was a farmer in all the Highlands who was as prosperous as Luran MacDhui. He had the finest herd of black cattle you ever saw, and nothing gave him greater pleasure than to sit and count them in the field of an evening.

One evening, though, he set about counting his herd, and was sure he made the tally short. Had someone been stealing his cows? A reiver from another glen would have run off a whole bunch of them, if not all. So was there a gap in the fences, or the dykes around his fields that his missing heifer had gotten away through?

The next day he went round all his property, fixing a bit of fence here and putting back a couple of fallen stones from a dyke there, but never a proper gap in them did he see. So that was not the answer.

The next night, he leaned on the gate and counted them all again, and to his astonishment and anger, he saw that yet another beast had vanished. The next day he went round his property again, but there was no explanation to be given by fences or dykes; they were all in perfect order. So what was to be done?

First thing in the morning, he questioned his cowherds, but none of them could explain the disappearances, and he trusted them as he would his own sons. There was only one thing to do: he would sit up and watch.

That night, he had all the cattle brought in to the field nearest his house, and he sat in the shadow of the byre. Hour after hour he watched, and nothing happened. The moon rose high in the night sky, and still nothing happened. The owls hooted and hunted, and bats flittered over the roofs and treetops, but still nothing happened.

Luran was very sleepy, and his head was beginning to nod, when he saw a troop of the Good Folk, the fairy throng come running and skipping and jumping up the field. They called one of the bullocks, and it rose unsteadily, and lumbered off, following them.

Luran leaped up from his hiding place, and ran as fast as he could after them, but they saw him coming, and were much faster than he was. They reached the foot of a mound called Tom na Shee, or the Fairy Hill, and a door opened in the hillock, through which the fairies and the bullock entered. It closed, and Luran could find no way in. Peching and gasping as he was with running, he went round the mound three times, taking care to go deiseil, or sunwise, knowing that to go widdershins, or anticlockwise round a fairy hill could mean nothing but trouble, and it seemed as though he had enough of that already. As he made his way home, a voice came floating through the air to him, saying: "Porage wi saut and butter! Porage wi saut and butter! That's what ye need tae run fast!"

This seemed like good advice to Luran, who at once embarked upon a diet of porage, with salt and butter, and took to running everywhere as exercise.

He kept this up for a year, and when his cattle started to disappear again, he watched and waited for the fairy folk to appear out of the mound.

Sure enough, one night, here they came, running and skipping and hopping and dancing. They called to one of the bullocks, and led it away. This time, Luran was a lot faster on his feet, and he managed to keep up with the fairy folk, but this time, running on the far side of the hazel hedge. When they arrived, he crept up close to the door of the Fairy Hill, which remained open, as the wee folk were not aware of his following them.

Inside, he saw a great party going on among the fairy folk, and his bullock provided the meat for the feast. They ate, and drank from beautiful silver goblets, singing and dancing, and having a wonderful time to themselves.

Then, gradually, their wee heads began to nod, and, one by one, they fell asleep.

Luran crept cautiously in among the sleeping fairies, taking great care not to trip over or awaken any of them. His bullock was gone, but what could he take in exchange? If he took more than the bullock was worth, he knew that he would never have peace from the fairy folk ever again. He gingerly picked up one of the silver goblets. No, that would not do. It was worth far more than the beast was worth.

But what about the kettle on the hob? That looked a serviceable utensil. Very carefully and slowly, he crept farther and farther in over the sleeping fairies, and unhooked the kettle from its place over the hob. Then, going as cautiously and carefully as he could, he made his way to the door. He stopped to look round, to make sure that none of them had seen him, and none had. They all lay sleeping sound. Luran turned to go home, but in doing so, the kettle hit the side of the door with a deep and resonant 'bong'.

The fairies were awake in an instant, and Luran took to his heels and ran.

He didn't dare run home, but where could he go? He ran through the bracken, he leaped through the heather, the fairy folk all shouting and swearing and cursing at him as he went. But how long could he keep it up? He ran over the ridge of the brae, his legs pounding and his heart thumping in his breast, his lungs feeling as if they were about to burst. The fairies still came on after him, showing no signs of being tired, and they were furious, promising all sorts of terrible revenges on Luran when they caught him.

Luran was sure that they would overtake him, and his life would not be worth living from that moment on, when a voice came to his ears, saying: "Luran! Run to the shore! Run to the shore!"

Luran remembered that if he crossed the tide-line, the fairies had no power over him there. He turned, and ran with all the speed he could muster, down the brae, over the machair to the sand dunes; over the soft, dry sand, down to the firm damp sand, and over the line of seaweed and driftwood that marked the tide-line.

Safe at last, he sat on the wet sand with his back against a rock, peching and gasping and wheezing, struggling to get his breath back, while the fairies danced with rage on the far side of the tide-line.

Luran summoned enough breath to shout: "Fair exchange, boys; fair exchange!"

Just at that moment, the sun raised a finger of light above the hills in the east, and all the fairy folk vanished. Luran wearily made his way home with the kettle, and never had any trouble with the fairy folk stealing his cattle ever again, and he kept the kettle that boiled the water almost before you poured it in, and his family still have it, and show it proudly to the neighbours whenever they come round for a wee ceilidh.

"Porage with salt and butter is a good meal, I am told," said the Dark Stranger.

"Indeed, I know of none better," said Shifty, "unless it was the apples of youth."

"Apples of youth?" said the Dark One. "I was not aware that such fruit was still in existence."

"Well, it was a long time ago that Uisna the Sage, the wise man of Erin, came across them, or at least, one, but not so long ago as all that, I'm told."

Uisna the Sage and the Apple of Youth

They say that in all the green land of Erin there was none wiser than Uisna the Sage. He was sitting one fine morning on the banks of a river, when he saw a sight that would puzzle and astonish most of us, but came as no surprise to Uisna: it was the sight of a figure looking like a fair and most beautiful man, all in white, walking on the water of the river towards him.

"Welcome to you, Mongan of the People of Dana," said Uisna. And indeed, the newcomer was one of the people of the goddess Dana. They had been great in the old days, but with the coming of the new people, they retired from view, and were to be seen only in the mists on the hills, and heard in the wind in the trees, but Uisna was privileged to speak to them face-to-face, on rare occasions.

"My greetings to you, Uisna the Wise One," said Mongan, "and a fairer day than this we have not seen in many a week."

"Aye, each day has its virtue, but this is a fine one, surely," agreed Uisna.

"Not so fine for everyone, though, in my observation," said Mongan.

"And who is so discomfited by the day as to bring you across the water to me?" demanded Uisna.

"This is good land, is it not?" said Mongan, by way of reply.

"It is all of that," replied Uisna.

"But if such land as this were starved of water, now, it would not be so grand, in my opinion."

"True for you," said Uisna, "but where is there land hereabouts that has not enough water?"

"A poor childless couple live on the far side of that hill," said Mongan, "and the spring that waters their land gives them nothing more."

"That is sad indeed," said Uisna, "but is there no remedy for this sad state of affairs? Does the rain not fall on them, as well as on other folk?"

"If it does itself, it is not enough for the land in this dry season. The remedy lies in the hands of a farmer whose land is to be found on the other side of the hill. He it was who put a great boulder up against the spring, to divert all the water from it on to his own property."

"Does this childless couple know why the land is left waterless?" asked Uisna.

"They do not, and even if they did, the strength of the man is not enough to shift the boulder. Indeed, if the situation is to be rectified, it must be by the hands of the farmer alone, and none but he."

"And is this farmer fellow amenable to reason? Can he not be persuaded to move the boulder?"

"He is a hard and stubborn man, with no wife to help him see reason, and no children to soften his obstinacy."

"Well," said Uisna, "it seems a hard case, and if the man will not bow to reason and compassion, I wonder what is to be done at all."

Mongan reached into the folds of his white robe, and produced an apple, which he handed to Uisna.

"Do you know what this is?" he asked. Uisna did, and he felt his mouth watering as he looked at it, and felt the aches and pains of his age groan and creak for relief, for this was an apple of youth. One bite of it would take seven years off Uisna's life, and if he were to finish the whole apple, he would be a young lad again, with all his strength and vitality, but better than that, he reckoned, he would know the things that an old man wishes he knew when he was young. It was a sore temptation to Uisna to gobble the apple up there and then!

"Ah, yes. Such things are greatly to be desired," said Mongan, as if reading Uisna's thoughts, "but one man's wish is another man's crying need."

"So it is," said Uisna, and put the apple away safely in the bag that he carried at his side.

"I think you will find a way to use the apple to restore things to their proper places," said Mongan, "and I would add this: as the years drop away from the one who eats such an apple, so does the memory of the years gathered through age. Thus, a man who becomes seven years younger does not carry with him the knowledge that he had before he ate it. Do you see?"

"I see," said Uisna. "I did not know that, Mongan."

"You know it now, and can use the knowledge, I think," said Mongan, and went his way, over the river, and away into the mists of the hills.

Uisna gathered his things and set off, first to visit the childless couple. The man sat outside their cottage, weaving a basket out of tough grass, while the woman was busy in the house.

"Peace on all here," greeted Uisna.

"And on yourself, and the blessing of God with it," replied the man.

"You seem to me in a poor case," said Uisna.

"Indeed we have seen better days," said the man, "before the land became dry."

"What will you do?" asked Uisna.

"If no quench comes to this drought, we shall have to take to the road, and beg our living," said the man, sadly.

"Good people have been driven to that before this," said Uisna.

"They have, and thank the Lord that we have no children to feed, or we would be in a terrible state entirely."

"Well, I wish you better fortune," said Uisna, and after speaking a blessing over the house, he went on his way.

A couple of hours' walk round the hill brought him to where a heavy-set, red-haired man stood leaning on a gate, looking out over a field of good barley.

"Your harvest will be good," said Uisna.

"Not good enough," said the man.

"Some round here complain of drought," said Uisna.

"I have taken precautions against that," said the man, "by the sweat of my brow and the strength of my arm."

"That is the best way," said Uisna, "but I wonder, would you show me now, how you did that?"

"I will. Follow me," said the farmer, and led Uisna up the hill to where the glen lay spread out before them, green in every direction, except where the poor childless couple had their piece of dry, barren land.

"Do you see this rock, now?" the man said. Uisna saw it. "I found that the water from the spring here was running down both sides of the hill, and I thought to myself that if all the water ran down to my side, I would have richer land than it was when I got it."

"And so you put the rock there?" said Uisna.

"With my own hands and a fierce heavy great lump it was, too!"

"I could imagine that just thinking about the work gives you an appetite," said Uisna, offering the fellow the apple that Mongan had given him, in spite of knowing that a couple of bites would make him young and lively again.

"Thanks," said the farmer, and took a bite. Immediately, seven years of age fell away from him, and a young, strong fellow stood, looking around him.

"You know," said the farmer, and his voice was younger, too, and more pleasing than his former gruff tone, "a fellow might make something of this land, with a bit of hard work."

"I think you are right," said Uisna. "How does that apple taste, now?"

The farmer took another bite, and another seven years just faded like the mist in the morning.

"It is indeed, a fine piece of land hereabouts," said Uisna, "and a man could make a good living from it, with hard work and dedication."

"He would," said the young man who now stood before him, "if that was his choice. But that's not the life for me."

"Oh?" said Uisna, "and what way of life are you following?"

"I'll be a warrior for the king, if he'll have me. Sure, it's the only life for a man."

"Glad indeed the king would be to have you, a fine healthy, strong fellow like yourself," said Uisna. "I'll bet a taste of that apple would not go amiss now!"

The young man bit into the apple again, and a further seven years melted away, and a young lad stood before Uisna, looking around him.

"Well, young fellow," said Uisna, "What are you up to today?"

"Just looking for something to do," said the boy.

"Oh, there's a job here, but I don't know if you're the fellow to do it," said Uisna.

"What is it?" the boy asked.

"Do you see this great rock, now?" asked Uisna. The boy did, and sure he could hardly miss it.

"That great lump of a thing is blocking the water from running down the hillside to the land over there, and the land is suffering because of it. Do you think you could move it, at all?"

"I'll have a try," said the boy, and spitting on his hands, he set to work to roll the great rock from its place.

At first it would not budge, but Uisna gave advice that the boy took up right away.

"Dig away at the bottom there," said Uisna. "Take a stick and dig away round the bottom of the rock."

It took a little while, but the boy was determined, and Uisna knew how to give the right advice and encouragement.

"I think I have it now," said the red-haired lad, and gave the rock a great heave with his shoulder against it. At last, the great rock rolled over, and the water began to flow down both sides of the hill again.

"Well done!" said Uisna, "fair play to you indeed! Now, after all that work, a taste of that apple would be welcome, I'll bet."

The lad took another bite, and a child stood where he had been. Hand in hand, Uisna and the child went down the hillside towards where the childless couple lived. A little way from the house, the boy said, "I'm hungry!"

"Here," said Uisna, "have a bite of this."

The wee boy bit the last of the apple, and now it was just a baby that Uisna gathered into his arms, and took to the couple.

"Good day again," said Uisna.

"Do you know this, I think it *is* a good day," said the man. "Can you smell that air?"

"There seems to be a bit more life in it now," said Uisna.

"I could swear there was," said the man, "just as it used to be. I believe the water is coming back to us. You can smell it in the air. But what's that you have there?"

"Ah, now this is a poor motherless child," said Uisna, "and it would be a blessing to good home to have a child like this. But I couldn't impose such a burden on you."

"A burden? Not at all," said the man, and he called his wife out.

"Ah the poor wee mite," she said, taking the baby in her arms. They agreed with all their hearts to take the child and rear him as their own, and that is what they did.

As Uisna went on his way, his old joints and bones nagged him for not having taken the apple for himself, but he told them to be satisfied that things had turned out for the best this way.

"I suppose that was as good a way of sorting things as any," said the Dark One.

"Och, old Uisna had many a ploy like that," said Shifty, "and the King of Erin was glad of his help in the old days, though he wasn't there to help the king when he met the cobbler."

"The great and mighty King of Erin had personal dealings with a humble cobbler?" said the Dark One. "You can't expect me to believe that!"

"Ah, but he did indeed," said Shifty, "and this was the way of it."

The Cobbler and the King of Erin

The King of Erin once had an argument with the Bishop of
Cashel. It seemed that the bishop had suggested that the king
was not as wise as he should be, though others said the cause
was something else. Whatever the argument was about, the
king was mighty sore about it, and threatened the Bishop with
swiping off his head, if he didn't appear at the palace at Tara to
answer three questions.

"What three questions, Sire?" asked His Grace.

"First, how heavy is the moon?" said the king. "Next, what
am I worth, and third, how long would it take to travel round
the world? There now; answer me those three questions by the
end of the week at Tara, and I'll forgive you the slight that you
have given me."

The bishop went away in a sombre mood, wondering how
in the world he would ever be able to answer such searching
questions as these.

On his way, he passed through a small town called Ballymuck
(which means the Town of the Pig) where he stopped to have
one of his shoes repaired.

"Though I don't suppose I'll be long in wearing it," he said
mournfully to the cobbler who had undertaken to mend it.

"Indeed? And why not?" asked the cobbler, sympathetically.

"The King of Erin has charged me to answer three of the
hardest questions a man ever asked another man," said the
bishop, "and if I can't answer them, it will cost me my head."

"That is a hard case, indeed," said the cobbler. "And would
you mind my asking what these questions were?"

The bishop told him, and the cobbler rubbed his chin
thoughtfully for a while, and said at last: "Suppose I went to the

king and answered them on your behalf? What would you say to that idea?"

"I would say," said the bishop, "that I would be mightily grateful to you, but how could you do it, you being a cobbler, and myself the Bishop of Cashel?"

"Now, I hope you can forgive my saying it," said the cobbler, "but many a one of my friends has remarked on my resemblance to yourself. If I were to dress up in your bishop's frocks and robes and suchlike fripperies, sure no-one could tell the difference between us, as long as we kept our hats on, for I have more hair on my head than you do, begging Your Grace's pardon!"

The bishop, after a few moments' thought, decided that the risk was worth taking, and so, when the time came for the bishop to answer the king's questions, off went the cobbler in the bishop's clothes, and indeed, there was nothing to choose for looks between himself and His Grace.

"Now," said the king, "are you ready to answer my questions?"

"I am ready to try," said the cobbler.

"Good," said the king. "Now, how heavy is the moon?"

"First, Sire," said the cobbler, "you'll allow that the moon has four quarters?"

"It has," said the king.

"And you will remember that four quarters make a hundredweight?"

"They do," agreed the king.

"Then it stands to reason that the moon weighs exactly one hundredweight!" said the cobbler, and the king was forced to agree.

"Very well," said the king, "now for the second question. What am I worth?"

"I can answer that exactly," said the cobbler. "You are worth twenty-nine pieces of silver."

"Why that?" the king demanded, surprised to have so exact a sum placed on him so quickly.

"The greatest man that ever lived was sold for thirty pieces of silver," said the cobbler, "and I think that you will be almost, but not quite, worth as much as Him."

"Good again," said the king. "But how would you answer my last question, which is: how long would it take to go round the world?"

"That's easy enough," said the cobbler. "Twenty-four hours."

"Again, a quick reply," said the king, "but how do you justify that answer?"

"Sure, doesn't the sun itself take just twenty-four hours to go round the world?" said the cobbler, and the king was mute with amazement.

Finally he said, "You are such a wise and witty fellow, but I wonder if you can tell what I am thinking?"

Now he was sure that he had his man at his mercy after all, even though it was a fourth question, and one more than the bargain agreed. But the cobbler spoke up at once, and said:

"I can, for you are thinking that I am the Bishop of Cashel, but in fact I am the cobbler of Ballymuck!"

So saying, he took off his borrowed mitre, and revealed a full head of hair, while the bishop was bald. The king's heart melted towards the cobbler and the bishop, and he forgave them both for the trick they had played on him, for after all, had the cobbler not increased the king's store of knowledge through his wise answers?

"Now," said the Dark One, "you can tell me tales of people who use their wits to get out of difficult situations, but it is not always so, my Shifty Lad! There comes a time, as I have mentioned to you this dark night, when even quick wits and cleverness are not enough."

"And that is true, too," said Shifty, "for there was a farmer in the Isle of Man who found that hard work is as needful as quick wits."

And quickly he began his next tale.

A Moon of Gobbags

There was once a huge giant living at the top of a hill called Sunrise Hill. This giant would wander over the island, being careful not to trample the houses of the people underfoot.

One day, he was in the neighbourhood of a place called The Lagg, when he felt something very rough and scratchy under his feet.

"What's this I can feel through my brogans?" he asked himself. "It's a queer kind of corn they do be growing in these parts!"

Of course, what he was treading on was thistles; a mighty bunch of them, for this farm belonged to a man by the name of Colcheragh, who was a terrible lazy man altogether. His house wanted thatching, but he would not climb up on to the roof to mend it; his cows wanted milking, and he was too lazy to go out and do it, saying that there was time enough for all that, and turn over and go back to sleep.

But here was this giant making such a row and a commotion that Colcheragh had to go out and see if it was a thunderstorm, or what was happening at all.

"Oh, it's yourself!" said Colcheragh, looking up at the giant.

"It is, and I'm wondering what class of corn this is at all that you have growing in your fields! Look at my brogans; they're all scratched through! What do you call this stuff?" and he snatched up a handful of thistles.

Now Colcheragh felt enough shame not to admit to letting weeds grow on his land, but not enough shame to stop himself from lying about it.

"Don't ye know that it's great good luck to have them growing on your land?" he said. "They belong to the Good Folk. You'll never lack for a soft bed if you have these growing on your land. A thistledown bed is the softest of all beds."

"Do you say so, now," said the giant. "Then it's fortunate indeed I am to meet you this day, for the rocks up on Sunrise Hill are hard and lumpy. Sell me seven bags of this thistledown, and I'll give you a heap of copper and lead. There are mines and caves are full of that class of stuff in some parts of the island."

"Well, when the time comes, I'll oblige you with pleasure," said Colcheragh, "but you'll have to wait till the right time for plucking thistledown."

"And when would that be?" asked the giant.

"The next moon of Gobbags, I'll be out there, plucking the thistledown," said Colcheragh.

"Moon of Gobbags?" said the giant. "What in the world is a Moon of Gobbags?"

"Ah, now! Don't tease me, Mister Giant me Friend," said Colcheragh. "You know fine what a Moon of Gobbags is. Just bring me your bag when the next Moon of Gobbags rises and I'll fill it for you seven times over. Now, I'll bid you good day, for I'm needing a rest after a hard day's work."

"See and don't leave any of the prickles in the bags when I bring them," said the giant, as he strode away, looking forward to a nice soft bed to sleep on at last. Colcheragh went inside thinking himself a wonderful clever chap, but there's an old saying among the Manxmen, that goes: "You'll never find a hole to slip through in a giant's pockets", which means that once a giant has hold of you, there's no escaping from him. Colcheragh's wife warned him of that.

"What will you say to him when he comes for his sacks of thistledown?" she said.

"He'll be coming for them at the next Moon of Gobbags," said the farmer, and there's plenty of time before that, I reckon, for I've never seen a Moon of Gobbags, and neither has the big fellow!"

So saying, he rolled over and went back to sleep.

Now the giant was in a state of great puzzlement and confusion. He knew all about Harvest Moons and Hunter's Moons, and had even heard a waif word about True Lovers' Moons, but no word had ever reached his ears about a Moon of Gobbags. So he made his way to his friend Ada the witch.

"That's the grand day," she said to him, "and mighty handsome you're looking in it, my great beauty."

"And it's yourself is looking very trim and tidy," said the giant in reply.

"And what brings you over to my bit on such a day?" asked Ada.

"I am in a great pickle of astonishment and bafflement," said the giant, "for I am trying to discover what a Moon of Gobbags is. I've been searching my memory for what a Moon of Gobbags might be, but nothing sticks in my mind about it at all, and I shan't have a soft bed to sleep on until the Moon of Gobbags. It's banjaxed I am entirely."

"A Moon of Gobbags?" said Ada, "why, you great lump, someone is taking a loan of you right enough. Take a broom and sweep all the sand off all the beaches in this island, and make a rope of seaweed to pull this island all the way from Malin Head to the Butt of Lewis, and when you've finished, you can search the sky for a Moon of Gobbags, for, my dear heart, there's no such a thing!"

"Do you tell me that!" roared the giant, and ran off in a rage to Colcheragh's farm.

"You're come too early," said Colcheragh, "for didn't I tell you that the thistledown wouldn't be ready until a Moon of Gobbags?"

"Ye did, ye impudent wee speug!" shouted the giant, and the noise was terrible. "Moon of Gobbags indeed! There's no such a thing! Now I'll be bringing my bag tomorrow evening, and you had better have the thistledown all ready for me, or else!"

And so saying, he stumped off with great stampings of his enormous feet.

"Well," said Colcheragh's wife, standing looking at him with her hands on her hips. "There's only one way to deal with this, my lad, and that's the quickest way. You'd better get those thistles pulled, and you'd better get a bend on doing it, too!"

Colcheragh dressed himself for work, and scratched his head and rubbed his chin, but there was nothing for it: he would have to do some work to get out of the hole he was in, and he would have to be quick about it, too. There wasn't enough thistledown there to supply the giant, and the breeze was blowing what there was here and there and all over.

So Colcheragh set to work pulling the thistles from off his land, and his hands were red raw and sore at the finish of the day, and the following day he ploughed his field until there was no sign of thistles, or where they had been growing.

At sunset, the giant came tramping over the fields towards him.

"I'll just be taking my thistledown and be on my way," he roared, but Colcheragh replied: "You're too late! The Good Folk have taken it all! I turned round for one minute, and here was my field all ploughed and the thistles away. Maybe if you hurry, you'll catch them up, for they went that way!"

The giant went trundling after the Fairy Folk, but he never caught them up, for they weren't there to start with.

"Now my lad," said Colcheragh's wife, "from this day onwards, you'd better not let a single thistle be seen on your land, or it's himself you'll have to reckon with, and his great big bag!"

Colcheragh learned his lesson all right, and from that time onwards put as much work into labour as he had done into avoiding it before, and there never was a cleaner, nor a tidier farmer in all of the Isle of Man.

"Giants can be tricky customers. And there's another farmer who was lucky in his choice of wife," remarked the Hooded Stranger.

"Right enough," said Shifty. "Perhaps he was another who watched how she ate cheese."

"And what has cheese, or how you eat it to do with the choice of a wife?" asked the Dark One.

"Have you never heard how canny men in Scotland choose their wives?" asked Shifty in surprise. "Why, they give a woman a piece of cheese, and watch whether she cuts away the rind with a lot of cheese, and she would be a wasteful woman; or they see whether she eats the rind and all, and she would be a greedy woman. If she pares the cheese right down, and just leaves a thin skin of rind, she's a canny and careful wife, such as the six silly fishermen had."

The Six Silly Fishermen

There were once six fishermen all named Angus. They were
all tall and each man had red hair. There was another called
Tommy, with dark hair, but he wasn't with them on the day of
this tale.

They were out one day fishing, and they caught a good catch,
and were well-paid for it with a purse full of silver. As they made
their way home, they wondered how they should best divide the
money amongst them.

"We'll need tae count it first," said Angus number one.

"Aye, that's the best plan," they all agreed, and they counted
the money out.

"Now we need tae see how many we are," said Angus the
second, and he began to count his pals: "One, two, three, four
five ... Wait a minute, where's Angus?"

"Ach, ye're daein' it all wrang," said Angus the third. "Let me dae it!"

So he counted all his pals. "One, two, three, four, five ... Ye're
right enough, there's one of us missing!"

"Stand back boys, and let a bit of light in on the subject," said
Angus the fourth, and he counted his pals all together, too, but
like his pals, forgot to include himself in the calculation, and so
came to one short.

"Angus is away!" said Angus the fifth.

"That's strange; I didnae see him go," said Angus the sixth,
and they all started shouting the name "Angus" as loud as ever
they could, to see where their missing pal had got to.

Well, of course, there was no reply, as they were all standing
there together.

"What if something bad has happened to him?" said Angus
the first.

"Ochone ochone, that would be terrible, just," said Angus the second.

"But what could have happened?" said Angus the third.

"Mebbe he fell down the well yonder," said Angus the fourth, and they all ran over to the well, and Angus the fifth leaned over the edge, down into the water, where his reflection looked back up at him from down the well.

"Och, look! There he is," he said, and waved to his reflection. The reflection waved back. "See, he's waving back!" he told the others.

"Well, we'd better get him out of there," said Angus the sixth, but none of them had arms long enough to reach.

"Here," said Angus the first, "I'll tell you what; Angus, you hold my ankles, and lower me down. Mind and dinnae drop me, now!"

So Angus the second held Angus the first's ankles, and lowered him down into the well, but still, he couldn't reach.

"Here, Angus, you take my ankles, and we'll be a man longer," said Angus the second and Angus the third held Angus the second by the ankles, while Angus the second held on to Angus the first's ankles.

But still they couldn't reach.

"Here, I tell you what it is," said Angus the fourth. "I'll hold Angus's ankles, and that way we'll get closer to him."

So Angus the fourth held Angus the third's ankles, while Angus the third held Angus the second's and Angus the second had hold of Angus the first's. So Angus the fourth had a very heavy weight to hold, as he was holding on to three men. But still they couldn't reach.

Now Angus the fifth stepped forward, and offered to take Angus the fourth's ankles, in the hope that they might get closer to the man in the well, but still they couldn't reach. So at the end of the day, Angus the sixth took Angus the fifth's ankles, as well as the weight of the other four, and extremely heavy they all were!

Angus the sixth was a very strong man, but he was beginning to find the combined weight of his pals a bit too much for his strength, but here they were, all hanging upside down in a well, and he daren't let go, or everyone would end up in the water.

"You're slipping!" he told Angus the fifth.

"Dinnae let go!" yelled Angus the fifth, and all the others yelled: "Dinnae let go!" And a loud wailing of "Dinnae let go!" came from the well from five dangling fishermen, while the man at the top did all he could not to let his pals slip.

Just then, their wives came back from getting the messages, and saw Angus the sixth looking pale and worried at the edge of the well.

"What are you doing, Angus?" cried his wife.

"I'm holding on to the other lads," he shouted back, as his grip grew more and more slippery.

"What! Are our men hanging down that well?" said one wife to the other, and all six women made their way across to the well, and yanked their men out one by one, with a lot of opinions from them about how silly it was to dangle down a well like that.

When the men were all out on the firm ground again, Angus the first said: "But here, what about Angus?"

"What Angus?" said his wife. "All the Anguses are here! Look!" and she counted them all: "One, two, three, four, five, six."

"Well," said Angus the second, "We must have rescued him after all."

And they all went home.

"Indeed, and none knows better than yourself what it's like to be hanging on for your life," said the Dark One. "Now, get to your feet, my Shifty Lad, for we must be moving."

"The tale was another about sensible wives," Shifty objected. "Of course a sensible wife is a blessing," he continued, "but there are other kinds, too, like the wife of the Cornish Blacksmith."

The Blacksmith's Wife and the Apprentices

In Cornwall, many years ago, there was a blacksmith, who took to wife a beautiful woman, and very pleased he was with her. One thing she brought with her to the blacksmith's house was an old bridle. The blacksmith told her to get rid of it, and get a new one, but she was very fond of this old piece of tackle, and would not part with it at any cost.

There was plenty of work for the blacksmith, but not so much that he could not manage it all himself, and so he was surprised when his wife advised him to take an apprentice. However, he did as she counselled him, and the apprentice was a bright lad who was quick to learn the trade. It was not long before the blacksmith's wife encouraged the blacksmith to take on another apprentice.

The first apprentice was a Christian lad who wore a silver cross round his neck, in memory of his mother, who had given it to him before she passed away. At first, the blacksmith's wife was very kind to the first apprentice, but one day, when she caught a glimpse of the little silver cross, she had little more to do with him. The new lad, though, she made up to and treated very kindly. The first lad noticed this, but was too sensible to worry about it.

As time went by, the first lad noticed that the second apprentice was waking from his sleep more tired than he was when he went to bed, and was growing paler and thinner by the day.

He said nothing about it, until one day, his workmate climbed out of his bed, and just collapsed on the floor.

"What ails you, Davey?" the first apprentice asked.

"I don't know for sure," Davey said in a weak, plaintive voice. "Every night someone whistles me down to the stable and puts an old bridle on me and rides me like a horse all night, all over the countryside to meet the witches down Polperro way. I'm all done up and done in from it, I can tell you!"

"Do they, now!" said the first apprentice. "Well now, you lie there, and I'll tell master you're sick. We'll deal with the business of riding later!"

That night, after the day's work was done, and the supper eaten, the first apprentice went and hid in the stable, and waited.

At midnight, he heard a sharp whistle, and saw a dark figure come into the stable and take the old bridle hanging there from a hook. He crept up behind the dark figure, and snatched the bridle away, and put it on the mysterious stranger's head.

At once, the figure became a fiery black horse, and the apprentice jumped on its back and rode the creature over the countryside, taking care to ride up steep hills and rocky places, and to and fro over ploughed fields, all night.

Just as dawn was beginning to break, he rode his magical steed back to the forge, and put new shoes on the horse, driving the nails in deep. Then he took the bridle off the horse, and ran back to his bed in the loft beside Davey's.

The next day, the blacksmith's wife took to her bed, sick. The blacksmith called for the doctor, though she insisted that she didn't need him. The doctor came and asked to take her pulse. She would not let him, and kept her hands well under the blankets. The two apprentices came in to see how she was doing while the doctor was trying to persuade her to at least let him shake her hand in greeting.

"Come now," said the apprentice, "you must let the doctor do his job," and he pulled the blankets back.

Under the blankets, the blacksmith's wife was hiding her hands, because they were shod with good iron horseshoes. She leaped out of bed, and her feet were the same, each with a strong iron horseshoe firmly nailed on.

"How on earth did this happen?" gasped the blacksmith.

"'Twas I gave her a dose of her own medicine," said the apprentice, and explained why Davey had been so pale and wan lately.

"Ah, ye can all go to blazes," said the blacksmith's wife, and she jumped out of the window, and ran away, never to be seen again.

The blacksmith was astonished and sad, but in time he married again, and his second wife had nothing of the witch about her, while the two lads in time became doughty blacksmiths in their own right.

❧

"Of course," said Shifty, "there are witches enough about the place, but mostly not as wicked as that one. Most of their spells and cantrips are used to cheat others and do themselves a bit of good, like the woman on the shore at Vatersay in the Western Isles."

"Well," said the Dark Stranger after a pause, "are you going to tell me about her?"

"Och well, it was this way," said Shifty. "You know that in the Western Isles the cows often come down to the shore? There was a day when some lads just back from the fishing saw a wifie that they were a wee bittie suspicious about, hanging about on the sand, with something behind her back. One of them managed to have a wee keek behind her, and saw that it was a tangle, which is to say a stem of seaweed. He crept up behind her, and cut the tangle in half with a knife, and milk flooded all over the shore. She'd been milking the cows, and keeping the milk all wrapped up in the seaweed tangle through a spell that she made. But she gained no profit from it that day. Others are far worse witches, mind you, such as the one that Michael Scott met after his graduation."

Michael Scott and the Witches

Not long after Michael Scott made his way from the tower where he had studied the hidden arts with Dòmhnull Dubh, or Old Hornie as some folk call him, he caught up with a couple of his fellow students, and the three went on together.

Their way took them through a forest, where, as the light grew dim under the thickness of the branches, they encountered a terrible white dragon, or worm, rearing up its dreadful head and roaring fiery breath at them.

Michael's two companions at once forgot all they had learned, and ran to hide in the bushes, but Michael stood firm. Raising his staff, he spoke a spell that froze the worm where it lay. Then, taking his sword, Michael cut off its head and left it lying in its own black gore.

The three of them went on their way, finally emerging from the forest and coming out on to the bare hillside. They came to a lonely cottage, and asked the old woman who lived there if they could stay there for the night. She let them in quite hospitably, and asked who they were and where they had come from.

The three of then were not keen to let on that they were graduates of the College of the Hidden Arts, but Michael's companions told her about the encounter with the worm, and Michael's bravery in confronting it.

"Tell me this," said the old woman, "did you keep the head, at all?"

"I did not," said Michael.

"Ah, it's a wonderful thing, the broth of a great white worm's head. Would you be so kind as to go back into the forest and fetch it for me?" she asked, and Michael felt that it would be a small return for her hospitality to do so small a task.

He set off, and within two hours was back with the head all wrapped in his plaid.

"The broth is a wonderful thing for keeping you healthy through the winter," said the old woman, and she put the head in a pot, and set it on the fire to boil and then simmer.

Now Michael Scott was somewhat curious about this interest that the old woman showed in the worm's head. His companions, he knew, would want no part of such a broth, but he was keen to know what value it was to her.

"I think I've an ague coming on me, good woman," he said to her when the time came to go to bed. "If ye don't mind, I'll just sit here by the fire and warm myself through to fight off the shivers and sneezes."

The old woman agreed, but said to Michael not to touch the pot with the worm's head.

The darkness fell, and all in the house were sleeping when Michael carefully lifted the lid of the pot, and, taking a wooden spoon, took up a little of the broth, and tasted it.

At once he felt a difference flooding through him! All that he had learned in the College of the Hidden arts amounted almost to no more than a pile of beans. Great and terrible knowledge flowed through him in a warm stream, and it was from that time on that he had the gift of prophecy, the knowledge of all heathen tongues, the knowledge of the language of the birds and the beasts, and much more besides. It was as if the learning he had gained before was a handful of seeds that had all blossomed into great and colourful plants and trees within his soul. But he also knew that he would have to be extremely careful how he used such wisdom as he now had.

When the cock crew in the morning, the old woman came down, and the first thing she did was to lift the lid of the pot, and take a generous spoonful of the broth. As soon as she tasted it, she shrieked with rage.

"Michael Scott, you have taken the virtue of the broth to yourself! My curse on you, and may you be torn to pieces!"

Then she uttered a spell that turned Michael into a hare, and set her vicious mastiff dogs on him.

Michael ran for his life, with the dogs on his trail, their hot breath warming the scut of his hare's tail. He knew that he would have to be safe from the dogs before he could speak the spell that would disenchant him, and bring him back to his former shape, but he could not do it while in mortal peril from the mastiffs.

All day he ran, dodging and weaving, doubling and leaping. At last, he found a drain, and ran into it, knowing that the dogs could not follow him in the narrow gap. He slithered and crawled to the far end, and crept out. He spoke the spell that changed him back and made his way stealthily back to the cottage. His friends had long gone by this time, but there was an eerie light shining from the house windows.

He crept closer and closer, and peered in through the window, only to see a great coven, or gang of witches, dancing round the table, led by the old witch woman, who was singing a song about her dogs tearing Michael Scott to shreds.

Michael flung open the door, and spoke a spell that froze the witches' hands on to the hips of the witch in front, so that they made a circular chain.

"Not torn to pieces yet, you old hag," he cried, "but it was a long dance your dogs led me! For that, you and your friends can dance a dance for me!"

He spoke another spell that made the witches dance in spite of themselves, and so powerful was it that none of them could speak a spell to break it. They danced and danced, crying for mercy, to be allowed to sit and get their breath, but Michael had no mercy for witches, and left them dancing.

"There's little trouble they can cause in that condition," he said to himself, and went on his way.

And some say that travellers tell of a house in the Border country where a chain of witches groaning for mercy still dances the day and night away, for ever.

"Mind you," said Shifty, "the witch might have turned him into something worse than a hare. Sure, witches themselves make themselves into hares when the need arises."

"Do they indeed," said the Dark One, "and no doubt you have a tale to tell on the subject, but it will have to wait, for we must be up and away."

"And up and away was what Malachi Mulqueen was when he encountered the hares," said Shifty, and launched into his story.

Malachi Mulqueen and the
Council of Hares

Malachi Mulqueen was a tailor, and he used to travel all round Ireland with his pins and needles and his lengths of cloth, and people would invite him in to hear the latest gossip, for no-one hears more gossip than a travelling tailor, and to get their best clothes mended, or new clothes made up.

One day, Malachi arrived in a small town where there was no business, and no-one wanting his services, and so he made for the inn, hoping to be put up for the night, but there was no room at all, for a group of priests had taken every room in the place.

"Is there nothing at all?" asked Malachi, and looked around at the folk who had taken up all the available space.

One of the priests, the oldest of them, turned to look at Malachi, and stared at him with one cold blue eye, and one blind, pale eye.

"You could try Gerry Cunningham's a little way out of town," said the landlord. "He sometimes takes in people for the night."

Malachi took directions from the landlord for how to get to Gerry Cunningham's, and trudged away up the road.

He found the place all right, and knocked at the door. It was a long time being answered, and finally, an old man, leaning on two sticks, opened the door, and asked what Malachi wanted.

"I heard that you might have room for a night," said Malachi.

"Oh, right enough," said the old fellow, and called to his wife, who came through from the back of the house, with a smile. A lovely young woman she was, and quite a surprise, for although it is not uncommon for an Irishman to marry a young wife when he is in his middle years, she looked young enough to be his grand-daughter.

"Can we make up a bed for this fellow?" wheezed the old man, and his wife seemed quite happy to do so, though Malachi thought that her eyes were a particularly chilly shade of green; like Connemara marble, he thought.

That night, Malachi could not sleep. He tossed and turned this way and that; he tried having his arms out of the covers, under the covers; he tried everything, but he could not get off to sleep.

Then, in the small hours of the night, he heard a noise like someone filling a metal bath with bucketfuls of water.

"That's what I need," he thought to himself, "cooling off! That would settle me."

He heard what he thought was someone climbing into the water, and then a splash, and a skittering noise, like claws across a stone floor.

Finally, just before dawn, he managed to fall asleep.

In the morning, he awoke, went downstairs and thanked his host and hostess, and went on his way.

Now, it chanced a few years later, and at exactly the same time of year that Malachi Mulqueen found himself in the same part of the country, and again, in the same case where work was concerned; nobody wanted his services. Again he made his way to the inn, but here were the priests again, taking up all the space in the inn. He ordered a small glass of whiskey to warm himself for the road, and, looking around, he caught the gaze once again of the cold blue and pale, blind eye of the old priest. Malachi raised his glasheen and drank the stern-looking man's health, but received no acknowledgment of the friendly gesture.

"Does the old fellow Gerry Cunningham still take in lodgers for the night?" asked Malachi of the innkeeper.

"Poor Gerry passed away a year ago," said the landlord. "And long before his time, too. He was a lot younger than he looked, you know. But I believe his wife might accommodate you, if you need a room."

Malachi wasn't sure about imposing on a young widow, but there was no other place to be had. So off he went up the road to the Cunningham house. Mrs Cunningham remembered Malachi, and took him in with a smile.

That night, Malachi couldn't sleep again. He tossed and turned, but couldn't get comfortable. And then, in the middle of the night, he heard the same sound of a metal bath being filled with buckets of water, the sound of someone climbing into the bath, and then the same splash and the skittering of claws across a stone floor.

Malachi got up and crept downstairs. There was no sign of anyone about, but there was the bath full of cool water, and it was a hot night.

"A cool bath will settle me," thought Malachi, and took off his clothes and climbed in to the cool water.

No sooner had he done so, when he became aware of strange things happening. His ears grew long; his nose began to twitch; he grew fur all along his limbs, and in a matter of moments, found himself transformed into a hare!

He leaped out of the water and ran out of the house, wondering what on earth to do in such a fix. He came at last to a hilltop, where there was a great congregation of hares of all shapes and sizes. In the centre of the group was a black hare, who looked around with one blue and one pale, blind eye.

"Are we all met?" said the hare with one blind eye.

"Aye, all here," replied the hares in chorus.

"Yet there is one here who has not been invited!" thundered the hare with the blind eye, looking right at Malachi. Beside him was another hare, who turned to look at him with cold, green eyes, the colour of Connemara marble, and she let out a screech and began to chase Malachi, ready to rend him with her teeth and claws.

Malachi ran and ran, leaping over streams and up hills and down slopes, until he managed to make his way back to the house where he had been staying. He leaped through the door, right into the bath of water, and rolled around. Jumping out again, he found he was his old self again. He ran up to his room and gathered his belongings, just as he heard the back door swing wide and a splash sound as of a furry body jumping into the water. Curses and swearing came to him from downstairs, as the witch, Mrs Cunningham, came chasing after him to put all manner of evil spells and suchlike on him. He climbed out of the window and ran, naked and clutching his clothes, across the countryside, until he was far away from that place, and he never went back.

But from that day onward, there was always a little patch of fur on the back of his neck that had kept dry when he jumped back into the water. He was somewhat ashamed of it, and always kept it covered with a scarf, and the proof of it is that his family still have the very scarf!

"A strange tale indeed," said the Dark Stranger, "and few there are who would credit it!"

"No doubt about it at all," said Shifty, "but the most unbelievable tale I ever had to tell was of a man I knew, a fat sassenach, who went skating on the ice one day. He went out too far and slipped through the ice. And if that wasn't bad enough, the ice was so sharp where he fell in, that it swiped his head clean off his shoulders! His body went one way under water and his head slid over the top, and they met again at another hole in the ice. It was so cold and frosty that his head was frozen back on."

"It is unlikely that he would survive such an accident," said the Dark One.

"Indeed he did," said Shifty, "at least, until that evening when folk were all sitting by the fire telling stories, and the sassenach sneezed, and he sneezed his head right off into the hearth, for the warmth had melted the join! The whole thing happened at Old John and Old Mary's house."

"And who were they?" asked the Dark One.

"They're the ones who got rich from the carelessness of the wicked Factor," Shifty explained, and told their story.

Old John, Old Mary and the Factor's Purse

John and Mary were very popular people in their part of the world, and everybody had a good word to say about them. They had grown-up children away in other places, some of them across the sea, but John and Mary still lived in the wee house that they had lived in all their married days, which was the house where John had been born and grown up himself.

Now as time drew on, and they both grew older, John, when he reached the age of ninety, would have times when he thought he was just a wee boy at school. At first this was very worrying for Mary, and a great pain to her, but these times only lasted a day at a time, and when John woke up the next day, he would feel very shamefaced about it, though there was never anything wicked or malicious in what he did in his second childhood days.

"Oh dear, Mary," he would say the next day, "did I ...?" and she would nod and say, "You did, John."

"Oh dear oh dear," he would say, and get on with the day's work, whatever it was; digging the peats for the peat stack, or planting potatoes in the lazy bed, with all the more energy for his excursions of the previous day.

One day, John woke up, and it had happened again.

"Time for school, Mammy," he said to Mary, who by now just sighed and made him up a play-piece of bread and jam and an apple, and off John went to school.

The schoolchildren were always happy to see John come to join them, for he knew lots of games that had almost been forgotten by this time, and he showed them Hunch-Cuddy-Hunch and Dreepin-

Aff-A-Dyke and other similar ploys and pastimes. The teacher was pleased to see John, too, for the children liked John, and took a lead from him, and John always tried to be a good pupil and set a good example. He knew the answers to lots of questions, and his old hand would shoot up to answer in class.

While John was at school, Mary had a visit from the Factor. Nobody liked the Factor. He was the man whose job it was to collect the rents and send them to the Laird, who lived far away. There were some who said that the Factor raised the rent without telling the Laird, and kept the difference for himself, and indeed, he looked a lot richer that he should for a man in his line of work. Here he came up the road on his fine horse, and knocked at Mary's door.

"Where's your man the day?" he asked as Mary fetched the rent money. Mary was too embarrassed to say that John was in his second childhood that day, and down at the school, so she told him that John was away working, which was true enough.

"Aye, it's a fine property, this," said the Factor, with a greedy look in his eye, and Mary knew that he was waiting for John and Mary to pass on, and he would put new people in and raise the rent considerably. She growled under her breath at the man, who was putting his big purse in his saddlebag.

Somehow, the Factor missed the saddlebag, and the heavy purse fell on to a clump of heather, without the Factor noticing, and he rode on his way.

John came home from school at the end of the day, hopping and skipping and full of songs from the schoolyard, when he saw the purse, lying in the clump of heather on the far side of the road from his house.

"Jings! Just look at this," he said. "Someone will be missing this! I'd better put it in a safe place." And the safest place he could think of was among the peats in the peat stack at the head of the house, which he duly did.

The next morning, he woke up, and his face fell.

"Och, Mary, I didnae, did I?"

"Aye, John, ye did," she said.

"Was I away tae the schule?"

"Ye were."

"Oh no. Not again!" he sighed. "Ach well, I'd better get aboot my work," he said, and went off to hoe the turnips.

While he was out working, Mary went to the peat stack to fetch some fuel for the fire, and she found the purse.

"Well, here a to-do!" she said. "Whit's this daein' here at all?" And she, too, thought that it would be best put in a safe place, but her choice was more grown-up than John's. She put it up in the roof among the thack, or thatch. Then she went off to get the messages, leaving John in the field working.

Not long after Mary left, the Factor came by in a great anxiety, all flustered and his collar done up wrong.

"John! John!" he shouted, "Have ye seen a purse, man? A gey big purse, full of money?"

"A purse?" said John, scratching his head. "A purse, big and full of money?"

"Aye, that's it, just! A muckle big purse full of money! Have ye seen it, man?"

John thought and thought, as though searching deep in the far depths of his memory, and gradually, a smile spread across his old face.

"Aye, I found a purse! And I put it in a safe place. Where was this now it was ...? Och yes, of course!"

Off John went to the peat stack to fetch out the purse, but it was away. Mary had put it in a safe place without telling John.

"I cannae understand it," John muttered to himself, "I'm sure it was here! Someone must have taken it ..." and he continued searching and muttering to himself.

"Come on, John, think man!" said the Factor. "When did ye put it there?"

"It was just after I came hame from school," said John.

"From school?" cried the Factor in a rage. "Why ye daft auld *botach*! That wis the best part of eighty years ago!"

And he jumped on his horse and galloped away, and was never seen in that part of the country ever again. And so John and Mary were left with a muckle big purse full of money that no-one came to claim, and when they finally passed away, it went, with the house, to their children, who were amazed to think that their parents were so rich.

"Of course," said Shifty, "a lucky find is not always so lucky, like Michael Scott's box."

"What box was this?" asked the Dark Stranger.

"Did you never hear of that?" said Shifty. "Well, Michael Scott found a box outside the witches' house that I told you about, and he took it with him while they were doing their everlasting dance. But with every step that he took, the box grew heavier and heavier, and when he tripped over a tree root, it slipped out of his hands and fell open. A great hoard of fairies came dancing out, saying, 'Gie us work! Gie us work! We are working fairies! Gie us work!'

"So Michael Scott set them clearing heather from the braeside, but they did that in seconds and came back demanding more labour. He set them to make a kerb of basalt to the River Tweed, and they did that in no time. Then he made them split the Eildon Hills into three, and they did that, too. Michael Scott knew that he would never be rid of them, and they would make his life a misery, so he set them to make a rope of sand and sea-foam across the mouth of the River Solway. 'But that's impossible,' they cried, 'the sea will wash it away!' 'Nevertheless' said Michael Scott, 'that is my command to you!' And away they went to do it, but they could never finish it, because the sea would roll in and wash it away. But you can see where they try every day, if you go down to the Solway strand. There are ropes of sand and sea-foam to be seen at high tide."

"The tide of your time is on the ebb, my Shifty Lad," said the Dark Stranger.

"Aye, and I'm bobbing on the waves like a wee curragh," said Shifty. "Just like when Uisna the Sage showed the men of Lochlann the meaning of fear."

And the next tale he told was this ...

Uisna the Sage and the Men of Lochlann

Uisna was sitting outside his cave one morning reading a book of deep knowledge, when a messenger came running up from King Feargus.

"The men of Lochlann are on the sea," panted the messenger, "and the king wants you to go to Scotland and warn the Scottish kings that he will need their help."

"Tell the king that I will go at once," said Uisna, and made ready to cross the Moyle Stream that separates Erin from Scotland. Uisna travelled in a wee boat of hide stretched over a wooden frame, called a curragh, and with helpful tides and a following wind, he was soon in the land of Alba, or Scotland, and making his way to seek audience with the kings, for in those days, there was more than one King of Scotland.

As the emissary of the King of Ireland, Uisna was welcomed and it was not long before he was making his way back to the shore to assure Feargus that the kings of Scotland would send their support against the men of Lochlann, though it was said that these men, with their golden, braided hair and long ships knew no fear.

Uisna decided that there was time enough for him to cast a hook in among the fishes before he made his way back to Erin, and soon had a bag full of fish for his supper, when he saw a fleet of long ships coming down from the north.

Knowing that it would be useless to try to outrun them, he paddled his curragh right up to the leading ship, and hailed the captain.

"Come up here," called the captain, "you can be our guide."

Uisna climbed aboard the long ship, bringing his curragh and his bag of fish with him on to the deck.

"Do you come to make war?" asked Uisna.

"We have come to take what we want. If that means war, then we are ready for it," said the captain, and smiled.

"Ah, now. That is an interesting thing," said Uisna, and he went aft, and leaned over the side of the ship, crooning a melancholy little song. The men of Lochlann watched him, but saw no harm in what he was doing. Then, one of them noticed that Uisna was talking to a dolphin, who was making a noise like laughter.

"What are you doing?" the captain asked.

"Oh, I was just saying to one of King Feargus's hosts of the sea that you were planning to make war on him."

"Oh?" said the captain, turning to the bosun, and sharing a smile with him. "And what did he say?"

"What did he say?" said Uisna, "Sure, what would he say, and him a dolphin? He just laughed at the notion."

"Well, maybe there won't be so much to laugh at," said the captain, a little crossly. But some of the sailors heard the conversation, and began muttering to each other that perhaps there was more to the strength of the armies of Feargus's than they had reckoned with.

Uisna just sat aft in the ship, and fed some of the smaller fishes that he had caught to passing herring gulls, one of which perched on the gunwale, while Uisna talked to him.

"Eh-heh-heh-heh," said the seagull. "Eh-heh-heh-heh-heh!"

Uisna spoke a little more, and the herring gull took off into the sky, shrieking his herring gull cry, that sounds so much like wild human laughter.

"Aaaaarrh haaaaarh haaaarh haaaarh!"

"What were you talking about now?" the captain demanded, uneasily.

"Oh, I was just telling one of King Feargus's hosts of the air about your plans to make war."

The captain turned away, but after a while, he turned back and said: "And what did he say?"

"You're a terrible man for wondering what animals and birds

do be saying!" said Uisna, irritably. "Sure they don't talk at all, not in human language."

"He seemed to understand you," the captain said rather sulkily.

"Oh, he understood me well enough. Didn't you hear the laugh coming out of him when I told him?"

The sailors were muttering among themselves now, rather more loudly, that maybe King Feargus was a stiffer proposition than they had thought. The captain told them to be quiet, and the murmuring died away.

Just then, the long ships were passing close to the coast of Kintyre, and the armies of the Scottish kings were on the march to Campbelltown to sail in aid of Feargus.

"What are those armies?" asked the captain.

"Army?" said Uisna. "Sure that's no army at all! King Coinneach has a rat in his pantry, and those are the men sent to kill it."

The bosun turned to the captain and said, "They are loyal to Feargus, I think?"

"Every man of them," said Uisna.

"What have we to concern ourselves with Coinneach's ratcatchers!" scoffed the captain. "We know no fear!"

"I would like to know what fear is like," said the bosun, laughing.

"You'd like to know what fear is like?" said Uisna. "Don't I have it in my bag, here?" And he held up his bag of fish.

"What! You carry fear in your bag?" said the captain.

"Just stick your hand in there," said Uisna, opening the bag a little way, so that the captain could get his hand in.

The captain reached his hand in, and felt something cold, wriggling, damp, with sharp edges here and there. When he drew his hand out again, fish scales covered the skin. He shivered, and would not meet the bosun's eye. The bosun tried, too, and he also felt the cold, writhing mass with the sharp edged bits, and found his arm covered in silver fish scales when he drew it out. He shivered, too, and rubbed his hand and arm to rid himself of the memory.

"The coldness, the wriggling, the sharp edges among the softness and the dampness; that's what fear is like," said Uisna. "Those shivers running through you, and the knocking of your knees; that's fear!"

The muttering of the sailors grew louder and more mutinous as they heard what Uisna was saying.

A dolphin popped his head above the water at that point, and made his laughing noise, and a herring gull flew overhead, screeching in mad merriment.

"Hmm," said the captain, "I think maybe we come back another time."

He gave the order to put about, and Uisna was bundled over the side into his curragh with his bag of fishes.

It was not long before the long ships of the men of Lochlann were small on the horizon, and Uisna cast his hook over the side among the fishes again before going back to report to King Feargus that an invasion from the men of Lochlann was no longer to be feared — at least, for a while.

"So you see, Uisna was a man who knew how to work a man's will against himself," said Shifty, "and he was not above doing it with his own king when the need arose; like the time when Feargus wanted to go courting ..."

Uisna the Sage and the Wooing of King Feargus

It happened one bright day in late spring that King Feargus was looking very pleased with himself, stroking his beard and trying little jig steps, as though making ready for a dance. Uisna the Sage, who was visiting at the time, saw these signs, and his heart sank. Feargus had taken a fancy to a girl again, and nothing but trouble would come of it.

"D'ye think now, Uisna," said Feargus, "that a man of my age might marry again?"

"True it is that men of your age have taken new wives," said Uisna, fearing the worst.

"That girl Áine, now; what is your opinion of her?" And he pointed to a girl across in the field, sitting milking the goats.

Now Uisna was really worried. The girl that Feargus had his eye on was a young and beautiful woman, with hair like spun copper and eyes the deep blue colour of the sea on a warm day, and as graceful as a swan on the lake. But she was engaged to be married to a prince from the west, Conal of the Swift Hand, so-called because of his prowess with a sword in battle.

Now Uisna dared not tell Feargus about this, for he knew that it would be a point of pride in the king to win the maiden's hand over a younger, more handsome suitor, and Conal was a handsome man, right enough.

"I think I will begin my wooing of that fair maid, Uisna," said Feargus, and smiled to himself as he went inside the castle.

"Now, how are we to deal with this," thought Uisna, and went to his cave. There, he took the hide of a bullock, and went and sat under a waterfall, wrapped in the bullock hide, in order to find inspiration, and this was the way of the wise men and sages in those days in that part of the world, and was called in the tongue of the Gaels *taghairm*.

Finally, he emerged from under the waterfall, and made his way back to the king's castle.

Feargus was very fond of feasting, and there was to be a great banquet that night, where fine food was to be eaten, and wine and mead was to be drunk. Uisna, who took no strong drink as part of his wisdom and the maintenance of his wisdom, decided that he would attend this feast and watch the king closely.

During the feast, Uisna made sure that the king's drinking cup was always full, and that he was draining it often. The result of that was that soon, the king had taken more than he was accustomed to, and more than was good for him. He stood, and leaned on the table, banging the board for silence with the handle of his knife.

"Silence!" he thundered, swaying where he stood. The room grew quiet to hear what the king had to say.

"A fine feast this is!" he shouted, and all shouted their agreement.

"But it won't be long before there's another feast, and that one will be even greater than this, because ..." he paused, and Uisna felt his heart tighten in his breast as he waited for the king to continue. "Because it will be a wedding feast!"

There were cries of approval, and much thumping the table, and some shouted: "Whose wedding will it be?"

Again Uisna held his breath, but the king just put his finger to his lips, and said: "Ask me no questions and I'll tell you no lies!" and he sat down again, grinning broadly like a schoolboy.

At last the feast came to an end, and Uisna helped the king to his chamber, where he fell across his bed, and was snoring soundly. Uisna tiptoed away, but did not go far. He wanted to be nearby when the king awoke.

The king did indeed awaken, and very sick he felt after his night's carouse. He sent for Uisna to give him something to lighten the load in his head and help him to walk steadily.

Uisna looked at the king, took his pulse, made him stick out his tongue, and looked carefully in his eyes. He tutted and looked concerned.

"What is it, Uisna?" asked the king. "You've seen a man after a night's carouse before."

"Ah, yes, Sire, I have, but this looks ..." he broke off.

"Looks what?" demanded Feargus. "Speak up man — Ooh, my head!"

He clutched his head and rolled on the bed in great discomfort.

"Tell me this," said Uisna, "Do you see spots before your eyes?"

"I do. What of it?"

"And are there occasional flashes, as if of lightning, when you move your head too quickly?"

"There are — Ooh! There they are again! The lightning flashes!"

Uisna tutted again, and walked up and down, stroking his beard thoughtfully.

"Tell me this now," he asked. "Does your hand shake when you hold it out?"

Feargus held out his hand, and it shook like an aspen leaf. Uisna shook his head in worry, and paced up and down the room.

"Will ye stand still, man, and tell me what it is that's on your mind!" Feargus tried to shout, against the throbbing of his head.

"What concerns me is this, Sire," said Uisna. "A man with a strong, healthy constitution like yours; a man who is as used to the wine cup as you are should not have these symptoms. No, there's something more worrying here."

"Well, what man?" Feargus demanded.

"I very much fear that you are about to suffer a bout of second childishness!" Uisna solemnly announced.

"Second childishness? Is it dangerous?" Feargus asked, his eyes bulging.

"Oh no, not at all," said Uisna. "It just needs careful handling. Now you must put yourself in my care. You will feel as if you've gone to sleep, and when you wake up, the bout will have passed, and all will be well again. You'll remember nothing of the attack."

"So you can give me something for it?"

"Indeed I can," said Uisna, "and I'll fetch it directly. All you'll need is careful nursing. I have just the person in mind. Just sit back and relax now. You've nothing to fear."

Feargus sat back, but relax he could not, until Uisna brought him something in a cup that he said was medicine, and was medicine of a sort, for it was a strong sleeping draught. Feargus drank it off, and fell asleep.

Uisna then sent for Áine, and asked her to take a large pile of babies' napkins into the king's bedchamber, and place them beside the bed. She was to go quietly, though, for the king was resting. This the girl did, and Uisna asked to stay close by, as he might need her services again soon. She was willing enough to perform such easy tasks, and remained within earshot of the king's chamber.

The next day, Feargus awoke, feeling refreshed and full of vitality. Then he remembered what Uisna had told him, and sent for him.

"Ah, there you are, Sire, and all restored to your grown-up self!"

"Did I ...? Was it ...?" Feargus asked. Uisna calmed his fears.

"You had the best nurse while you were back in your babyhood," said Uisna, and went to the door and called Áine. In she came readily.

"Áine my dear, will you take those napkins away again? We shan't be needing them any more."

"Of course," said Áine. "Are you feeling more yourself now, Sire?"

Feargus nodded sheepishly, and as soon she was out of the room, he said to Uisna, "You don't mean that *she* was the nurse you found for me?"

"She did her job perfectly," said Uisna.

"You mean she saw me ... in that state?" Feargus squeaked.

"If she's to be your wife, Sire, there should be no secrets between you, I think," said Uisna sternly.

"But ... No, no! The whole thing's impossible. How could she take me seriously as a man if she's seen me in that awful state? No, the thing is off!"

"Oh, is that how Your Majesty is thinking?" said Uisna. "Well, if such is the case, perhaps it is better then, after all, that she goes far away from here. Yes, you are quite right! Perhaps far to the west."

"Indeed, you're right," said Feargus. But where?"

"It should be somewhere that we can find a husband for her, to take her mind off the whole episode," said Uisna. "What about Conal of the Swift Hand for a husband, now? Would he suit?"

"The very man!" agreed Feargus.

"Ah, but you'd be wanting to settle a decent dowry on the girl, after all she's done for you," said Uisna.

"Of course, of course. The very thing," said Feargus.

And so it was. Conal and Áine were married, and Feargus gave a rich dowry to accompany them home to the west, after the wedding feast, which, after all, Feargus had promised his household at the last feast. But this time, Feargus drank sparingly, and remained sober, if not solemn, and indeed, enjoyed the wedding feast as much as anyone else there.

"A proud king is a bad king for his people," said the Dark Stranger, "and a vain king is a danger to the country."

"Rhitta of the Beards was such a king at first," said Shifty, "or so the Welsh and Cornish people and the Breton people of France say."

And he began the tale.

Rhitta of the Beards

There were, once upon a time, two kings among the twenty-eight kings of the people of Britain; one called Nyniaw and the other Peibiaw. They were proud and boastful men, and would gather to show off their riches to each other.

"Have you ever seen such flocks and herds?" said Nyniaw, "or such smooth grassy pastures?"

"It's plain to see that you haven't seen much of the world," said Peibiaw, "for I have flocks and herds as numerous as yours, and greater still, and my pastures are smoother and richer than anything you show me here."

"Admit that you have never seen such land and animals as I have here!" said Nyniaw.

"Ah, but that I have, you see, and they are all mine, and I have seven times more of them than you have, and pastures, too!" answered Peibiaw.

Nyniaw turned away in a sulk, and then turned back with a crafty smile on his face.

"Come back to me here after sunset," he said, "and I shall show you a greater and richer pasture than you have ever seen!"

"Very well, I shall!" replied Peibiaw, and twitched his cloak around his shoulders as he left.

He returned that evening after sunset, and Nyniaw took him to the top of a hill, as the stars came forth and shone in all their colour and brilliance.

"Now," he said, "have you ever seen such a broad and rich pasture as that?"

"Where?" asked Peibiaw.

"Why," said Nyniaw, "the whole broad sweep of the

heavens, of course. All of it, as far as the eye can see, as far as the ear can hear; it all belongs to me!"

"Very good," said Peibiaw, "and just as good are the herds and flocks that graze there, and they all belong to me!"

"What herds? What flocks?" Nyniaw demanded, bridling.

"Why, the stars, man, the stars!" returned Peibiaw. "They are all my wool-rich flocks and my milk-rich herds, and there, see yonder my silver white shepherdess."

"What shepherdess, where?" Nyniaw said.

"Why, man, the Moon, of course," said Peibiaw. "Look, there she is, leading the flocks and herds to where they find the best nourishment."

"They shall not feed on my pasture!" cried Nyniaw.

"Ah, but they shall!" cried Peibiaw.

"Never while there is breath in my body!" cried Nyniaw.

"While there is strength I my arm, they shall!" said Peibiaw.

Soon the two kings came to blows, and as this was not enough to settle the business, they brought out their households to support them, and this led to more fighting, and more, until there was open warfare between the kings, and lands laid waste, and a great destruction brought to the land.

The king in North Wales at that time was a giant by the name of Rhitta. The news was brought to him of the strife between Peibiaw and Nyniaw, and he laughed scornfully at the foolishness of the two.

"I shall put a stop to this nonsense," he said, and led his army to where Peibiaw and Nyniaw were squaring up on the battlefield with what remained of their men.

Rhitta strode up to the two kings, and said, "Enough now of this foolish strife!" And he took a sharp knife and cut their beards off, all in a piece, and took them away with him to make a cap.

"Now you know better than to call the pastures and flocks and herds of heaven yours, when it is well-known to all, and plain to be seen, that they belong to me!" he said, and left the two kings bare-chinned and humiliated.

The other twenty-five kings of Britain gathered together in a solemn council, and agreed, one with another, that Rhitta was wrong and too arrogant and haughty in his treatment of Peibiaw and Nyniaw, and so they decided to march against Rhitta with all their armies.

Rhitta was not a whit dismayed by the approach of the kings and their armies, and in his giant's wrath, fell on them like a great hurricane, felling men and horses in his wrath, until he had all the twenty-five prisoners bound with stout ropes before him.

"Now, my fine fellows, proud as you were, you are humbled before me," said Rhitta, "and as I already have a fine cap of beards, I shall take yours to make myself a cloak!"

So saying, he set about cutting off each king's beard with a sharp flaying knife, and he sewed them together to make a cloak. However, when he was finished, he found that there was a gap above the hem that wanted a beard to finish it off neatly.

"I can find no rest while my cloak is incomplete," said Rhitta, and paced the land, cracking his knuckles and grinding his teeth.

The news came to him one day that there was a new king in the south by the name of Arthur.

"At last! I can complete my cloak," said Rhitta, and sent a messenger to Arthur, whom he found washing his sword after slaying a Cornish giant.

"Rhitta the king wants your beard," said the messenger, "and he invites you to offer it to him with all speed."

Arthur did not even look up from his task, but replied to the messenger, "Thank Rhitta for me for his kind invitation, but I think my beard is well where it sits now. But if he wants a beard for his cloak, tell him I can think of a better one for that purpose."

The messenger hurried back to Rhitta to bring Arthur's message, and Rhitta at once gathered nine of the biggest giants in his family to meet Arthur.

They gathered on a hilltop looking down into the valley, and saw a flash as of lightning running across the land.

"What is that?" asked Rhitta.

"That is Arthur's spears being raised in readiness for your coming," said the messenger. Then a wonderful sweet smell was borne on the wind to where Rhitta and his giants waited.

"What is that smell?" asked Rhitta.

"Arthur's men are drinking mead of the sweetest in honour of the battle that is to be," said the messenger. A great sound as of thunder crashed through the air.

"What is that sound?" asked Rhitta.

"That is Arthur's men, shouting in anticipation of the victory that Arthur will win," said the messenger.

Then Arthur stepped forth.

"So, Rhitta," he said, "I hear that you want my beard. Here it is. Will you came and take it?"

"Or what about mine?" cried Kay, Arthur's seneschal and foster-brother, and his beard was black, and square as a spade.

"Or mine," offered Uchdryd Cross-Beard, whose beard was forked like an adder's tongue, and all of Arthur's men gave a great shout, and the horses reared and the ground shook beneath them.

"What shall we do in the face of this host?" asked Rhitta, and his giant lords all agreed: "It is clear, Sire, that we must yield!"

Arthur called from the ridge where he stood. "There is a beard here that will mend the gap in your cloak!"

"And whose is that?" cried Rhitta.

"Your own," answered Arthur, and led the advance against the giants. The giants yielded to Arthur, and Uchdryd took a bone-handled flaying knife and cut Rhitta's beard away, all I one piece, and it exactly fitted the place by the hem of his cloak, and it was thick, with black and white hair.

Thereafter, whenever people looked out on a snowy night, they would remark: "The snow is as thick as Rhitta's beard!" And those who did not know who Rhitta was were told how his beard was made to mend the gap in his own cloak.

"That was in days long ago and far off," said Shifty, "but not as far off as the time when Sarah Finlayson was courted by a water-horse, or kelpie. They are very dangerous and bad-minded fairies, between ourselves. That was in the days before we had iron pots, and all our cooking was done in clay pots that the womenfolk made with their own hands."

"Well, and what became of Sarah Finlayson?" asked the Dark Stranger.

"Well, she was boiling water in a wee clay pot, you see," said Shifty, "and the kelpie came to her in the shape of a man, but couldn't disguise his snuffling way of speaking. 'It is time for you to go courting, Sarah Finlayson,' he snuffled. 'Just a little time yet,' said Sarah. The kelpie came a little closer, and said in his snuffling, horse-like voice, 'It is time for you to go courting, Sarah Finlayson!' But she kept watching the water in the clay pot. 'Not just yet, a little time yet,' said Sarah. Still the kelpie came closer to her, and closer still, speaking in his snuffling voice, saying, 'Time for you to go courting, Sarah Finlayson!' And Sarah knew that if he came too close, he would snatch her up and gallop away with her into the water, and she would be drowned. 'Come, now, Sarah Finlayson,' said the kelpie, 'it is time for you to go courting.' But just then the water boiled, and Sarah threw it at the kelpie, and it hit him between the legs, and he ran off howling."

"And it is time for you, too, Shifty my lad," said the Dark Stranger, "so rise and come with me."

"Ah, it seems my fortune has deserted me," said Shifty, not moving from where he sat. "Perhaps I was not taken upstairs out of the room where I was born."

"Such is the custom in your country, I believe," said the Dark Stranger.

"It is," said Shifty. "Or, if the house has no upstairs, or loft, then we set a chair outside the door, and the midwife steps up on to that from the room where the child is born."

"You have many such customs, I think," said the Dark One.

"Och yes," said Shifty. "You must never rock an empty cradle, and ill befall any cat or dog that jumps over a cradle with a bairn inside it! Of course, as any tailor will tell you, other places have other customs: the tailor who visited the town of Dumfries, for instance."

And, though the Dark One smote his fist on the wall impatiently, Shifty began his next tale.

The Tailor and the Rich Man of Dumfries

There was a tailor who visited the town of Dumfries, where a rich man had a fair daughter who was of an age to be wed, but seemed to have no inclination to do so. In the end, the rich man offered his daughter's hand to any man who would take her off his hands, but of course, he meant a rich man like himself, not a poor man, such as the tailor was.

The tailor came knocking at the rich man's door, for he had heard that the man needed a pair of trews.

"Indeed, I can make you a pair of fine trews," said the tailor, "and I would be proud to take your daughter off your hands, too!" For he had heard that the man wished to marry his daughter off before she grew too old for marriage.

This was too much for the rich man, who could see that the tailor was not as wealthy as he himself was. At first he was minded to throw the cheeky man out, but then he had another plan.

"Yes," he said, "I shall let you marry my daughter, on this condition: If you make me these trews down in the old chapel yonder, at midnight, I shall give you my daughter's hand."

"And there's a bargain," said the tailor, and shook hands with the rich man, knowing that there would be more to the job than just sewing a pair of good trews. However, he took a candle and a tinder box to light it, and his cloth and needles and threads, and made his way to the chapel.

Towards midnight, he set to work by the light of the candle to make the trews. He took great care, making the stitches so small that they could hardly be seen, and he sang happily as he worked.

But then midnight struck, and the church bell had hardly stopped chiming the midnight hour, when a great flagstone in the chapel slid slowly back, and a monstrous head appeared, with eyes looking directly at the tailor.

"D'ye see this great head o' mines?" asked the creature.

"I see that, but I'll sew this," said the tailor, and carried on working on the trews.

The monster poked his head out farther, so that all his mouth was visible, including his sharp, yellow fangs.

"D'ye see these great teeth o' mines?" the monster asked.

"I see that, but I'll sew this," replied the tailor.

The monster heaved and shuffled until one huge hairy shoulder appeared in the gap in the floor.

"D'ye see this great shouther o' mines?" said the creature.

"I see that, but I'll sew this," said the tailor, working all the faster in the guttering candlelight. The monster shuffled and heaved, and pulled his other great hairy shoulder into view.

"D'ye see this ither great shouther o' mines?" he growled.

"I see that," said the tailor, "but I'll sew this," and the stitches grew longer as he worked faster and faster.

The monster heaved himself a little farther out of the hole, until his horrible hairy chest was visible.

"D'ye see this great brave breist o' mines?" the monster said.

"I see that, but I'll sew this," said the tailor, his needle flying like a gnat.

"And d'ye see this great belly o' mines?" the monster growled, bringing his awful pot belly over the edge of the hole.

"Aye, aye, I see that," said the tailor, "but I'll sew this." And the needle flew faster and faster, and the stitches grew longer and longer.

"D'ye see this great leg o' mines?" roared the monster, pulling one leg out of the hole.

"I see that, but I'll sew this," said the tailor, his needle flashing like lightning through the cloth.

"And d'ye see this other great leg o' mines?" the monster said, just as the tailor was biting off the last thread, and the trews were finished.

"Aye, I see them fine," said the tailor, "but I wish to see no more, thank you," and he blew the candle out, and ran to the door.

He ran and ran as fast as he could to the rich man's house, and ran in through the door, locking and barring it fast behind him as he did so. The monster, running after the tailor, was not quite quick enough to catch him, and as monsters cannot enter houses into which they have not been invited, he brought the wall of the house a great smack with his monstrous hand, and left the mark of his five dreadful, claw-like fingers there, and they can still be seen to this day.

The tailor handed over the trews, and the rich man had to agree that they were a fine garment, and that they had been made under the conditions that he had set, and so he called out his daughter.

"This brave man has made me these trews in the chapel at midnight," he said. The girl looked at the tailor in astonishment and admiration.

"He must be a brave man, as well as a handsome one," she said, looking the tailor up and down.

"Would you take him as a husband, though?" the rich man asked.

"He's a better proposition than all those skinny-malinky long-legged students that you show me from the University," she said, and so the bargain was concluded, and the tailor wed the rich man's daughter, and they were as happy together as the day is long, which in Scotland, in the summer time, is long indeed. Of course, in the winter, the days are shorter, and they had their ups and downs, but they passed for a happily married couple wherever they went, and whoever met them.

"And I daresay," said Shifty, "that he kept his wife as well as Sandy Harg kept his wife. She was such a beautiful girl that the Good Folk wanted to take her away to Fairyland and keep her there."

"How did Sandy Harg know that?" asked the Dark Stranger, for indeed he had an appetite to learn all that he could about the ways of men and women.

"Sandy was coming home one night from fishing, when he saw some of the People of Peace, that is, fairy folk, busy on the shore with twigs and moss and such like. He called to them: 'What are you doing?' and they called back: 'Making a wife for Sandy Harg.' So he ran home as quickly as he could, and clasped his wife to him, and forbade her to open the door that night to anyone. Well, near to midnight, there was a chapping at the door, and his wife wanted to open to see who it was, but Sandy wouldn't let her go. The chapping went on and on, and there were calls to open the door, and sad and desperate they sounded. Sandy Harg's wife wriggled and squirmed in his arms trying to go and open for the poor body at the door, but Sandy wouldn't let her go. The noise of chapping and knocking went on until the dawn, and the cries for them to open up and help a poor body, but still Sandy held tight to his wife. Then, when the cock crew, it all stopped.

Later, in the broad daylight, Sandy went to open the door, and a thing made all of moss and twigs in the likeness of his wife came falling in through the doorway. Sandy took it and burned it on a fire, knowing that the Good Folk had left it there, hoping that Sandy would think it was his wife while they huckled her away to their own country, and there are very few I've heard of that went there and came back, like Thomas the Rhymer."

And, though the Dark Stranger hissed his displeasure at yet another delay, Shifty began the tale of True Thomas, and the Dark One listened in spite of his impatience.

Thomas the Rhymer

Thomas Learmont, the Laird of Earlston was a man of great learning. He loved books and poetry and music, and the world of nature was another of his great loves, which was unusual for the times he lived in. He kept a garden, and encouraged the birds to come and sing in the branches of his trees, and fed the small creatures that came in with the food that they liked.

One fine morning in May, he left his Earlston home and went out into the spring sunshine to enjoy the colours and scents of the season. He sat at the foot of a great tree in the shadow of the Eildon Hills, a tree known as the Eildon Tree, and took in the scene before him: the spring flowers, the new young leaves on the trees, the birds busy in the branches and the sound of the stream of the Huntly Burn purling by.

Suddenly, he became aware of a horse and rider moving through the woods towards him, though he heard no sound of hooves. Seven hunting hounds ran before the horse and rider, but were silent as they ran.

The horse was a fine grey palfrey, and the rider was the most beautiful lady that he had ever seen. She was all in green silk, the colour of the spring grass, and she wore a velvet cloak of the same colour. Her golden hair hung loose about her shoulders, but it was kept from masking her lovely face by a shining diadem of precious jewels. She carried a hunting horn and a sheaf of arrows.

The grey palfrey had a saddle of ivory, which the lady sat with easy grace, and the saddle cloth was of scarlet satin. The stirrups were of crystal, and the reins were hung with little bells, that tinkled a strange music.

Behind the horse and the lady ran seven greyhounds on a leash, to match the hunting hounds running before.

As they approached, Thomas could hear that the lady was singing a strange song. She looked so queenly and her dress and apparel were so magnificent that he thought he was in the presence of the Queen of Heaven, and he threw himself on to his knees, clasping his hands in prayer.

"No, Thomas," she said, "you must not kneel to me. I am not the Queen of Heaven, though queen I surely am. The Good Folk call me their sovereign, and Fairyland is my realm."

Now Thomas was a wise man, and well-schooled, and he knew that those who have dealings with the People of Peace rarely come out of it to their advantage. Yet such was the beauty of the lady, and her manner so calm and stately, that he was enthralled by her, and fell under her spell to the length that he begged her for a kiss.

She bent from the saddle, and bestowed a kiss on Thomas's lips, and as she did so, a dreadful change came over her. Even as Thomas watched, her golden hair turned to grey, and her young features became lined and pale. Her fine dress and cloak turned to the colour of ashes, and her diadem to a circlet of bone.

She laughed to see poor Thomas's dismay.

"I am not so fair to look upon now as I was," she said, "but you have had a kiss from the lips of the Queen of Fairyland, and so my servant you must be for seven years."

Thomas begged and entreated her to free him from this terrible bargain, but nothing would move her.

"There is no help, Thomas," she said, "and my servant you must be. Now, climb up here behind me, for the time is passing that I can linger here."

Terrified as he was for what lay before him, Thomas mounted behind the lady, and the grey palfrey ran with the speed of the wind, until the land of mortal men was left far behind them, and they arrived at a place that seemed to Thomas like a bare, barren desert, stretching as far as the eye can see.

"Now Thomas," said the lady, "dismount. Come and lie with

your head in my lap, and I shall show you things hidden from the eyes of mortal men."

Thomas did as he was bid, and sat with his head resting on the lady's knee, and the landscape changed as he looked. Three roads were now plainly to be seen. One ran broad and straight, so that no-one would lose his way on that path. The second was narrow and winding, and thorns and briars grew in great hedges on either side, stretching their branches across the path, so that none who tried that way would find it easy. The third was different again, winding up a hillside with bracken and heather and yellow whins; a pleasant path for any.

"Now," said the lady, "I shall tell you about these three paths. The first road, that is so broad and straight, leads to an end of sorrow and bitter regret for all who take it, though many take it, for it looks so easy. The second road, beset by thorns and winding all the way is the royal road of righteousness, and hard as it is to travel, it is the only one that leads to the City of the Great King. The third road, the bonny road that you and I shall take is the one that no mortal knows. It leads to Elf Land, and there we shall travel.

"Now, take heed, Thomas, and mark me well. You must speak no word in Elf Land, unless you speak it to me as my servant, or else you shall never see Earlston again, for no mortal being who moves his lips and tongue to speak in Elf Land can ever leave."

They mounted the palfrey again, and began to mount the path up the bonny braeside, with heather and bracken and yellow whins on either side, but on the far side of the brae, the path went downwards, into a deep chasm, and the way grew darker and darker, and the sound of rushing water filled Thomas's ears. The air in the chill gloom was dank and heavy.

The palfrey then plunged in to the cold, rushing stream, and Thomas could feel the water rising above his feet, and then up to his knees. He was in terror lest he fall and be drowned in that place, where no daylight penetrated. He fell forward in a faint, but always had a tight grip of the lady's cloak, or else he might have fallen and been lost in that cold, dark stream.

But now the darkness diminished, and the light began to grow stronger, until they emerged into bright sunshine. They rode through an orchard, where rich and luscious fruit grew that Thomas had read of in books, but never seen: dates, figs and other things grew plentifully among others that he knew, such as apples and pears. He was so hungry and thirsty that he longed to take some of this fruit, and reached out a hand to pluck some of it, but the lady turned and said, "Touch nothing here, Thomas. It is not safe for you. Soon I shall give you an apple, but touch nothing else, or you will remain here for ever."

They rode on, until they came to a tree that was wondrously small, though laden with apples. The lady reached down and plucked an apple from this tree, and gave it to Thomas.

"This I shall give you, and welcome you are to it, Thomas," she said: "And this fruit we call the apples of truth. Whoever eats the fruit of this tree cannot tell a lie."

Thomas ate this apple, and for ever afterwards, no lie ever passed his lips, and he was known as True Thomas by all who met him.

There was not much farther to go after this. The lady showed Thomas a magnificent castle on a hillside.

"That is my home," she said, "where the Lord of Elf Land lives, and all the nobles of his household. I must warn you that his temper is never certain, and he has no liking for handsome young gallants seen in my company. Say no word to anyone, and I shall tell them all that you are dumb."

Then the lady put her hunting horn to her lips, and blew a great blast. As she did so, a change came over her again, and once more she was the beautiful lady that Thomas had first seen in the Eildon woods, all in the rich apparel that she had worn. He, too, had changed, for instead of his hardy country clothes, he was now wearing a fine suit of brown cloth, and satin shoes on his feet.

Servants came running from the castle, and Thomas slid down unobtrusively from the palfrey, and passed into the castle with no notice taken of him.

Strange scenes met his eyes in the palace. Lord and ladies danced in the great hall, while others all dressed for hunting came and went bearing deer killed in the chase. Cooks came and went to prepare these beasts for the banquet. Thomas passed among the splendid-looking nobles and ladies of the castle, seeing how they danced and the rare quality and colours of their dress. So rich a scene he had never witnessed and every corner displayed something new and strange.

For three long days Thomas watched and marvelled at all he saw, but then the Queen rose from her throne overlooking the great banqueting chamber, and she said, "It is time to mount and ride, Thomas, time to mount and ride, if ever you wish to see Earlston again."

"But lady," whispered Thomas, "you spoke of seven years! I have only been here three days!"

She smiled, and said, "Three days, Thomas? Time passes quickly in Elf Land. It is seven years since we first met under the Eildon Tree. Now make haste, for every seven years, an evil spirit comes to Elf Land and chooses one of our followers to take back to the Place of Darkness, and I fear that he will choose you, so come with me and mount and ride."

Thomas and the lady mounted the grey palfrey once again, and they returned the way they had come, until once more they found themselves under the Eildon Tree, with the Huntly Burn rippling by.

The lady then bade Thomas farewell.

"Wait, my lady," called Thomas. "Won't you give me a parting gift, something that only you can give me? Otherwise, none will believe that I have indeed been in Elf Land with you these seven years past."

The lady smiled, and said, "I have already given you the gift of truth, Thomas, but now I give you the gifts of prophecy and poetry, so that you will be able to foretell the future, and tell it in verses of your making. I shall also give you this," and she gave Thomas a harp of rich and elegant workmanship. "Now farewell, my friend Thomas," she said. "Some day perhaps, I shall return for you."

So saying, she vanished away among the trees.

Fourteen years passed, during which time Thomas earned the reputation of telling the truth always, and his verses and harping were heard with delight. Some called him 'True Thomas' and others called him 'Thomas the Rhymer'.

The time came when Scotland and England were at war, and the English army was camped along the banks of the River Tweed. Thomas, the Laird of Earlston, summoned the Nobles and Barons leading the Scottish armies to a great feast. As they wined and dined, he played his harp for them, and sang songs of long ago, and songs that told of Elf Land, and the noble company felt that they had never heard such fine singing.

That night, the sentries of the camp around the castle saw a strange sight; two snow-white deer, a buck and a doe, were walking down the road beside the camp in the moonlight, showing no fear of the soldiers camped about them. So strange a sight was this that it was decided to send for Thomas of Earlston.

"Aye, send for Thomas, send for the Laird of Earlston," was the cry.

A messenger was sent to awaken Thomas and tell him of the wondrous sight. Thomas shed a tear at the news.

"It is a summons from the Queen of Elf Land," he said. "I have waited long for this, and now it has come."

He went out, and, instead of saying anything to the men who had woken him to explain, he walked straight up to the hart and the hind, who seemed to greet him. Then they all three set off down a steep bank into the River Leader, and disappeared into its waters, for the river was at that time in full flood.

They searched and searched, but they found no trace of True Thomas. The country people always said that he had returned to Elf Land, to the lady whose servant he had become as soon as he begged a kiss of her beautiful lips.

"Mind you, that was not the last that was heard of Thomas the Rhymer," said Shifty, "as the tale of Canobie Dick tells."

And at once, before the other could interrupt, he began to tell the tale of ...

Canobie Dick

There never was a cannier nor a braver man in all the bonny south land of Scotland than Canobie Dick. Folk said of him that if a thing was to be done, Dick would do it, and fearlessly. He dealt in horses, and drove a hard bargain, usually to his own advantage. He travelled all round the Eildon Hills and Bowden Moor; the lands that Thomas of Earlston knew well, and, it was said, King Arthur and his knights, as well. Some even said that Arthur and his knights lie sleeping under the Eildon Hills, waiting for the call in time of their country's peril.

Such tales were of little interest to Canobie Dick. The past was of no consequence to him. He was a man who dealt in the here and now, and looked always to the future.

One day, Dick was leading a string of seven horses in the region of the Eildon Hills, when a man of great age, white-haired and bearded, accosted him, and asked the price of the horses.

Canobie Dick looked at the stranger; his clothes which were of a fashion long gone, and his long beard and white hair, and was sure that he would be able to make a good bargain.

After some haggling, they agreed on a price, and the stranger reached into the pockets of his old clothes and fetched forth some gold coins, which he handed over before taking the horses and leading them away into the mists of the evening.

Dick looked at the coins in his hand, and was amazed to see that they were of a kind that were no longer in circulation, all stamped with bonnets and unicorns, the likes that had long passed out of use. Still, the coins were of good gold, and Dick reckoned that in gold alone, what he held in his hand was worth more than half again the value of the horses that he had just parted with.

Before he left, the old man settled with Canobie Dick that he would bring good horses to him, but always at the same spot, and always at night, and each time, Dick should come alone. Dick agreed to these conditions, and promised to return soon with good horses.

Over the weeks that followed, Canobie Dick returned often with good horses for his mysterious customer, and always received good payment for them, but always in the old coinage of bygone days.

Now, one thing for which Canobie Dick was well-known was his thirst. He always liked to settle a bargain with a drink at the buyer's expense, and his customers, knowing this, always provided good wine or ale to seal the contract, but no such carouse had he ever had with the old man of Bowden Moor. So the next time he went with a string of horses to meet the old man, he asked him whether he would take him to his home, and celebrate the sale with a drink.

The old man looked closely at Dick through the darkness of the evening, and said that indeed, he would take him to his dwelling, if he was not afraid to come. Canobie Dick prided himself that he feared no man living or dead, and could see no harm in the idea of following his client to his home.

"He must be a brave man who follows me home," said the old man, "but if your courage fails you at what you see, you'll rue it until the day you die."

"My courage has never let me down yet," said Dick, "and I don't see why it should fail me now. Lead away, sir, and I'll follow."

The old man turned, and led Canobie Dick along a narrow path for a long way, until they fell under the shadow of a low hill that was known in the country thereabouts as 'The Lucken Hare' and was said to be the abode of fairies and elves, or some said, witches danced there, and made their terrible contracts with the Evil Kingdom. But Canobie Dick was not the man to be afraid of such things, and strode on unabashed. However, he was astonished to see the old man turn down the path into a cave, for Dick had never seen or heard of a cave being there at all.

He paused at the entrance, and the old man, looking round, said to him: "Now is your chance to turn back, Canobie Dick. I warned you that your courage would be tried to its limits if you followed me."

Dick said merely, "I was just trying to remember the entrance to this cave, so that I should know it again."

"Time enough to see if you'll find it again," said the stranger, and led Dick further down into the depths of the earth.

The way became so dark that Dick could see nothing in front of him, and if the old man had not offered him his hand to hold, he would have lost his way for sure. After some time, however, they saw a light before them, and towards this they made their way.

Dick soon found himself in a great underground chamber, lit with flaming torches that threw flickering shadows on the walls and floor. All along the sides of the chamber were a row of stalls where horses were waiting, saddled and bridled. Each horse was coal black, and as Dick looked, he saw that beside each horse was a knight, all in black armour, lying asleep, but with a drawn sword in his hand.

Nothing moved in the chamber, other than the flickering shadows. The horses were still; all lay as if under a deep enchantment. No noise came from the horses or their sleeping riders; everything was motionless and silent. Dick, for all his bravery, began to feel an eerie chill creeping down his spine. His knees became unsteady, and fear began to steal round his heart.

The old man led Dick to a table, where there lay two objects; a sword of old and curious workmanship, and a hunting horn, the like of which Dick had never seen before.

"Now," said the old man, "have you ever heard tell of Thomas of Earlston, also known as True Thomas, or by some as Thomas the Rhymer? He was the man who was taken to Elf Land, and came back with the gifts of true speech and prophecy, given to him by the Queen of the country of the People of Peace."

Dick nodded, unable to speak, for what was the old man

doing asking him of a man long vanished from the haunts of men in this strange and uncanny place?

"I am that same Thomas," said the old man, "and since you are a brave man, I have brought you here to try your courage. Now, do you see these things here, this sword and this horn?"

Canobie Dick saw them clearly, and nodded again.

"He who blows the horn and wields the sword shall be the true king the length and breadth of this island of Britain," said Thomas. "But now, mark me well, for all depends on your courage now how the adventure will befall. The task will be light or weighty, depending on which you take up first, the sword or the horn, and know that it is I, True Thomas that tells you so."

Dick hesitated. He was, as a man of action, drawn to the sword. But how if there were unseen spirits in the chamber? They might think that to wield the sword was the sign of a challenge, and he would not want to stand alone against a host of such creatures.

Therefore, his hand fell on the horn, which he raised to his lips, and blew a tentative blast which was no more than a weak and feeble note, echoing in that great chamber.

What a result it had! At once there was a great stirring among the sleeping knights, who at once rose from their sleep, and mounted their coal-black horses with cries of warlike ferocity. The horses plunged and reared, and all was the din of a great host making ready for battle.

Canobie Dick, now terrified that these knights should make him their enemy, dropped the horn and reached for the sword, but before he could touch it, a great voice sounded echoing through that underground hall, saying:

> "Woe to the coward, that e'er he was born,
> Who drew not the sword before the horn."

Then came a mighty rushing whirlwind that swept him along the passage out of the cave, and dropped him on to the cold hillside, where he fell, tumbling and rolling over and over, with sharp stones and pebbles falling all about him all the way to the bottom.

The next day, he was found by some shepherds, and to them he told all that had happened, but his life was not long in him once he had told his tale, and the breath was out of him for ever as he closed his eyes for the last time on the cold hillside.

"A good tale to end on," said the Dark Stranger, "and now, my Shifty Lad, no more tales, for we must be up and away."

Shifty's mouth was dry with all the talking he had done, but if there was to be any hope for him, he had to keep talking until the first light of dawn. He scooped into the palm of his hand a few drops of cold rain water, and let them trickle into his throat. The night was at its darkest now, and Shifty could scarcely see beyond the top of the tall tower.

"Wait a wee while," he said, "for my limbs are stiff and cold. I'll be with you directly, but while I warm myself for the journey we must make, I'll tell you the tale of a poor fellow, and what happened as he walked home one night."

"No! No more time for tales now," said the Dark One. "Up with you, Shifty Lad, up with you!"

"It is a very short tale," said Shifty, "and soon told."

"Now, I'll tell you what it is, Mister-Shifty-My-Friend!" said the Dark Stranger, hissing through his hard, cold teeth as he spoke. "You are telling me these tales because you hope to pass the time until first light. You are trying to be clever, my Shifty Lad, but now *I* have a tale for *you* about a fellow who thought he was clever, and a great one for humbugging, and I'll tell it to you quickly now, before we make our journey. And make it we shall, mark my words! So listen to me a wee while, and get yourself ready as I tell it, for the last long journey."

The Gifts of the Three Beggars

A man and his wife were so poor that they had no resources in the world other than what the man could earn as a day-labourer, moving from place to place, in search of work.

One day, the man, whose name was Jimmy said to his wife: "Make me up my dinner now, for I'm away to look for work in the morning."

She made him as good a dinner as she could, and laid out his cleanest and hardiest clothes for working, and the following morning he set out in search of work.

On his way, he came to a bridge, and tripped over a loose stone.

"The devil break my neck if ever I pass this way again!" he said, and went on his way.

He found work on a farm, and worked for four years, faithfully and hard, never taking a penny from the farmer until the time was up, and he set off with his pay in his pocket and a bottle of beer that he soon emptied, but he kept the bottle.

On the way, he came to a crossroads, where a poor beggar sat.

"You are coming from a rich part of the country," said the beggar.

"Rich enough to pay me fifteen pounds for my work," said Jimmy.

"Then perhaps you can help me," said the beggar, "for I am a poor man, as you see."

Now, Jimmy knew poverty, and was willing to part with five pounds to help the poor fellow. The beggar gratefully received the money, and said: "What is the thing you wish for most in this world?"

"Anything that I desire," said Jimmy, "and to have the money to pay for it in my pocket, and that anything that troubled me to have shut up in this bottle here in my hand."

"You shall have what you wish, Jimmy," said the beggar, and Jimmy passed on his way.

Farther down the road he met another beggar, who also asked for alms. Jimmy was too kind-hearted to refuse, and handed over another five pounds.

"Now," said the second beggar, "what would you like most in the world?"

Jimmy stroked his chin and thought. Finally he said: "Anyone or anything that gave me trouble, I'd like him shut up in my bag here, until I gave him leave to come out again."

"That is a wish that I'll grant you, Jimmy," said the beggar, and Jimmy went on his way.

It was not long before he met a third beggar, and gave away the last of his pay to the poor man.

"And what do you desire in this world?" asked the third beggar?"

"Well, you know," said Jimmy, "I have an apple tree at home, and I am plagued by the boys in the neighbourhood coming and taking the apples before I get a chance to pick them. I should like for anyone who touches my apple tree to stick there until I give them permission to leave."

"Your wish is granted, Jimmy," said the third beggar, and Jimmy went on his way home, wondering how strange it was that so many folk knew him, and he had no idea who they were!

His way took him to the very bridge where he had stumbled on his way out, and who should spring up from a thorn-bush by the roadside but the devil. This was not Auld Hornie, Dòmhnull Dubh, but a rather inferior sort of devil. But devil he was for all that.

"Here you are at last, Jimmy!" said the devil.

"I didn't expect to meet you here," said Jimmy, "or anywhere else, come to that."

"Don't you remember on your way here, you said 'the devil

break my neck if I ever pass this way again'? And here you are, so I am ready to do what you said, and break your neck."

"Come ahead and try," said Jimmy, and the devil sprang at him, but Jimmy cried out: "Into my bag this minute!" And the devil had to go, thanks to the second beggar's gift.

Jimmy went on his way, and saw some women washing clothes at the riverside.

"I'll give you five pounds to give my bag a thrashing," he said to the washerwomen, and he could afford it, because of the first beggar's gift. The women laid on the bag with the big sticks they used for beating the dirt out of the laundry, and complained that the bag was as hard as the very devil.

"Aye," said Jimmy, "It's the devil who's in it!" And the women laid on harder still.

A little farther down the road, Jimmy came to a blacksmith's, and offered five pounds to the blacksmith to beat his bag on the anvil with his heaviest hammer. The smith set to work with a will, and beat so hard that a hole appeared in the bag.

"There's a hole in your bag," said the smith, "shall I beat it more?"

"Aye," said Jimmy, "thrash away, for it's the devil that's in it!"

The smith laid on even harder, and when the devil put his eye to the hole in the bag to see when the thrashing would stop, the smith took a hot iron from the fire and poked it in the hole, which is why the devil is half blind to this day.

However, the devil has some powers of his own, and as Jimmy went on his way, the one-eyed sprite burst the bag and made a swift escape.

Three months later, he came for Jimmy, wearing a patch over one eye.

"Say your prayers, Jimmy," he said, "for I've come to take you away, and no arguments."

"Come back tomorrow," said Jimmy, "I've work to do about the place."

"No, it has to be today, and right now," said the devil, "so get ready."

"Let me just have one last apple from my tree," said Jimmy. "In fact, if you get it yourself, I'll be with you directly."

The devil went to pick an apple, but stuck to the tree, and Jimmy gave him no permission to leave.

Seven years later, Jimmy went gathering firewood for his wife to light the fire, and chanced to take the very branch that the devil clung to. The one-eyed fellow gave a leap into the air and took hold of Jimmy by the collar.

"I have you now," he said, "and there's no help for you my lad, but you must come with me!"

"I can see there's no help," said Jimmy, "so won't you have a last drink with me before we go?"

After seven years stuck to an apple branch, the devil had something of thirst on him, and agreed.

Once the bottle was empty, the devil grabbed Jimmy by the throat. But Jimmy managed to say: "Into the bottle with you!" And the devil had to go, because of the first beggar's gift.

Time passed, and Jimmy's wife gave birth to a fine young son, and Jimmy took a bottle down from the shelf to fill it up with good ale to celebrate. It was the bottle with the devil in it, and as soon as the bottle was uncorked, the devil jumped out, and made off as fast as he could, being very wary of anything to do with Jimmy this side of the grave, and indeed, all his might is on the far side of it.

Jimmy had his bottle filled, and went off in search of a godfather for his son.

On the way, he met a priest.

"God salute you, Jimmy," said the priest. "And where are you going this fine day?"

"I'm looking for a godfather for my son," said Jimmy.

"Let me be his godfather," said the other.

"I shan't give him to you," said Jimmy, "for you only work one day in the week, and you don't do much on the one day that you do work."

And so the priest went on his way.

The Bishop met him next, and saluted him.

"Where are you going this fine day?" asked the Bishop.

"I am looking for a godfather for my son," said Jimmy.

"Let me be his godfather," said the other.

"Indeed, I shan't give him to you," said Jimmy, "for you have godchildren enough all over the countryside as it is."

And so the Bishop departed from him.

And now, who do you suppose met Jimmy next? It was none other than I myself, sent on the instructions of the one-eyed horny fellow, who would not risk another meeting, as all his power is on the far side of the Veil of the World, and he can be cheated and humbugged on this side.

"Make your peace with the world and all in it," said I, "for you are to come with me."

"Let me just baptise my son," says Jimmy, "and I have yet to find him a godfather."

"Whom will you have as godfather for your son?" I demanded.

"Why, none better than you yourself," said Jimmy. "For it's you that shall leave him the longest alive in this world."

"And so the baptism took place, and Jimmy came away with me as soon as it was finished, for there are some who cannot be cheated or humbugged, and I am one of them. And now the last tale of the night is told, so, again, up with you now, my lad! No more talk and no more tales, for I am tired of the sound of your voice, and will hear it no more."

During this story, Shifty's eyes had opened wide. A strange, wild hope was growing in his soul; a hope that he hardly dared to give shape in his mind, yet there was an important question to be asked.

"Wait — wait a moment," he stammered at last. "Where did this adventure take place?"

"In your own land," said the Dark One. "In Scotland." And he took Shifty's wrist in a cold, hard grip.

"And was Jimmy's wife, your godson's mother; was she called Morag?"

"Aye, she was," said the other, mounting on to the wall at the edge of the tower and dragging Shifty with him.

"And are there any marks by which you'd know this lad, your godson?" asked Shifty, pulling back from the Dark Stranger's relentless grasp.

"If you must know, there was a mole in his left oxter," said the Dark Stranger, and Shifty's heart leaped in his breast.

With his free hand, he pulled the shirt from his left armpit, and showed a dark mole there the size of a summer raindrop on a smooth flagstone, just visible in the gloom against his pale skin. The Dark One stared at the mark, and his grip on Shifty's wrist loosened.

"Was it like this one?" asked Shifty.

"Aye, very like," said the Dark One, and his tone had softened with wonder.

"Then I think you are my godfather," said Shifty, pulling his hand free from the cold grip, "for my father was a day-labourer in Scotland, and he died at my baptism, and my mother is called Morag, and you are to leave me long alive!"

As he spoke, the cock crowed. The Dark Stranger turned his gaze hard on Shifty, his eyes seeming now to burn with frosty rage.

Shifty skipped to the far side of the tower, away from the Dark One, and, as he did so, he saw the streaks of dawn light spread across the eastern sky.

"Look," he cried, "the first light of dawn! And it was your own tale that kept us here till the morning light! Ah, it's a good godfather you are to me, after all! And did you not know me?"

"If the meeting at the Bridge of Baile Cliath was made at your baptism, I would have known you," said the Dark One, "but it was a curse made at the churchyard gate." He continued, as if to himself: "So that was the secret of why I was bound to listen to your tales! It was an old *geis* made at your baptism! And I never knew you! It looks as though you have told your tales and talked your way out of my hands this time," he said, "but next time I come, I shall be no stranger to you. You shall know me again, just as I shall know you.

And mark you this, my Shifty Lad," he went on: "Your mother said that you would end your days of thievery on the Bridge of Baile Cliath. Well, so let it be. Let her words be the saving of you, and let your thievery end there. But if you ever steal or thieve so much as a pin — nay, if you steal so much as the *daylight from a room*, I shall come for you. I shall have left you long enough alive at that moment, and there will be no tale-telling that will save you then, my fortunate godson!"

So saying, he spread his great dark cloak, and leaped from the tower. Shifty rose to see where he fell, or where he flew, but there was no sign of him.

In the tower there was a trap door, and Shifty lifted it. It led to a winding staircase, down which he went, until he came out in a courtyard of the king's castle. In the courtyard was a bench, where he sat, shivering with cold and fright, until he passed out.

When he came to, it was in a warm bed, and the princess was sitting by the bed.

"We were afraid we had lost you," she said, smiling warmly, as relief and love lightened her worried face.

"I was close to being lost altogether," said Shifty, "but I have learned one thing this night, and that is that my days of thievery are over."

And so they were. Shifty became a trusted advisor and later a minister for the king, and even persuaded him that he would be a fitting son-in-law.

Shifty and the princess were married, and a long happy life they had together, and their children never tired of their father's stories, told around a warm fire in the long winter evenings, or on journeys to far places in the kingdom.

One day, long after the night on the cold tower, Shifty was looking out over the green fields from a window in the castle, as the princess sat sewing.

"Come away from the window," said the princess. "You're taking all the light."

And that is where our story at last comes to an end.

Some Gaelic and Scots Words in the Tales

Stoor	dust
Oxter	armpit
Stramash	fuss, violent chaotic situation
Reiver	cattle rustler
Peching	gasping, panting
Machair	low-lying land (often close to the sea-shore)
Cantrips	spells, magic
Cailleach	old woman
Botach	old man

Celtic Wonder Tales

And Other Stories

Ella Young

A collection of tales from Ella Young's classic re-telling of Celtic stories, selected from Celtic Wonder Tales, The Wonder Smith and His Son, The Tangle-Coated Horse and The Unicorn with Silver Shoes.

www.florisbooks.co.uk

A Rosslyn Treasury

Stories and Legends from Rosslyn Chapel

P.L. Snow

P.L. Snow has for many years been gathering the stories that are represented by the numerous carvings inside and outside Rosslyn chapel. Many of the carvings, eroded by the years or damaged by vandalism during the Reformation, have been lovingly restored over time. They are eloquent illustrations of the biblical, historical and legendary tales that they represent.

This book traces themes of transformation and metamorphosis through inward endeavour, and will be fascinating for anyone interested in stories from the beginnings of the world, Ancient Egypt, the Holy Land, Celtic myth and Scottish history.

www.florisbooks.co.uk

The King of Ireland's Son

An Irish Folk Tale

Padraic Colum

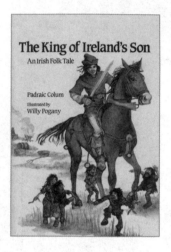

A born story-teller, Padraic Colum's prose holds the natural music of the spoken voice. Humour, poetry and action spring into these tales from the ancient lore of his native Ireland.

The King of Ireland's son sets out to find the Enchanter of the Black Back-Lands where he meets the Enchanter's daughter, Fedelma and is betrothed to her. He loses her and his adventures to find her again lead him to the Land of the Mist, the Town of the Red Castle, and the worlds of Gilly of the Goatskin, the Hags of the Long Teeth, Princess Flame-of-Wine, and the Giant Crom Duv.

www.florisbooks.co.uk